T0328926

The High Tide of Empire

Second Edition

LACTOR Sourcebooks in Ancient History

For more than half a century, *LACTOR Sourcebooks in Ancient History* have been providing for the needs of students at schools and universities who are studying ancient history in English translation. Each volume focuses on a particular period or topic and offers a generous and judicious selection of primary texts in new translations. The texts selected include not only extracts from important literary sources but also numerous inscriptions, coin legends and extracts from legal and other texts, which are not otherwise easy for students to access. Many volumes include annotation as well as a glossary, maps and other relevant illustrations, and sometimes a short Introduction. The volumes are written and reviewed by experienced teachers of ancient history at both schools and universities. The series is now being published in print and digital form by Cambridge University Press, with plans for both new editions and completely new volumes.

Osborne	*The Athenian Empire*
Osborne	*The Old Oligarch*
Cooley	*Cicero's Consulship Campaign*
Grocock	*Inscriptions of Roman Britain*
Osborne	*Athenian Democracy*
Santangelo	*Late Republican Rome, 88-31 BC*
Warmington/Miller	*Inscriptions of the Roman Empire, AD 14-117*
Treggiari	*Cicero's Cilician Letters*
Rathbone/Rathbone	*Literary Sources for Roman Britain*
Sabben-Clare/Warman	*The Culture of Athens*
Stockton	*From the Gracchi to Sulla*
Edmondson	*Dio: the Julio-Claudians*
Brosius	*The Persian Empire from Cyrus II to Artaxerxes I*
Cooley/Wilson	*The Age of Augustus*
Levick	*The High Tide of Empire*
Cooley	*Tiberius to Nero*
Cooley	*The Flavians*
Cooley	*Sparta*

The High Tide of Empire

Emperors and Empire AD 14-117

Second Edition

————

Translated with commentary by
BARBARA LEVICK
University of Oxford

 CAMBRIDGE
UNIVERSITY PRESS

Shaftesbury Road, Cambridge CB2 8EA, United Kingdom

One Liberty Plaza, 20th Floor, New York, NY 10006, USA

477 Williamstown Road, Port Melbourne, VIC 3207, Australia

314–321, 3rd Floor, Plot 3, Splendor Forum, Jasola District Centre, New Delhi – 110025, India

103 Penang Road, #05–06/07, Visioncrest Commercial, Singapore 238467

Cambridge University Press is part of Cambridge University Press & Assessment, a department of the University of Cambridge.

We share the University's mission to contribute to society through the pursuit of education, learning and research at the highest international levels of excellence.

www.cambridge.org
Information on this title: www.cambridge.org/9781009383691
DOI: 10.1017/9781009383677

First published 2023

A catalogue record for this publication is available from the British Library.

A Cataloging-in-Publication data record for this book is available from the Library of Congress.

ISBN 978-1-009-38369-1 Paperback

TABLE OF CONTENTS

Acknowledgements

I should like to express my gratitude to Dominic Rathbone and David Standen for helpful suggestions for improvement. It is also a great pleasure to acknowledge the help and generous advice of Grace Simpson, Philip Kenrick, Hedley Pengelly and Greg Rowe. But in particular I should like to thank Pauline Hire for all she has done throughout to improve the text and commentary.

*

In the course of this book I have included various passages which I also used in *The Government of the Roman Empire. A Sourcebook*, 2nd edn, published by Routledge, London and New York, 2000.

The following translations appear unchanged (*GRE* passage number followed by LACTOR equivalent in bold type):

17: **34**; 22: **176**; 27: **148**; 35: **35**; 38: **12**; 58: **109**; 64: **114** (partial overlap); 84: **99**; 89: **98**; 95: **125**; 101: **27**; 111: **156**; 112: **164**; 126: **175**; 131: **182**; 150: **211**; 151: **102**; 160: **107** (partial overlap); 161: **150**; 165: **192**; 173: **119**; 177: **121**; 183: **158**; 184: **155**; 193: **161**; 206: **142**; 220: **190**.

The following passages are in fresh translation:

4: **84**; 77: **229**; 81: **86**; 99: **43**; 103: **91**; 119: **180**; 122: **174** (partial overlap); 149: **77**; 159: **108**; 171: **124** (partial overlap); 181: **201** (partial overlap); 188: **157** (partial overlap); 191: **154**.

I am grateful to Messrs. Routledge for their permission to use this material, and for permission to draw on maps 1–5 in the same volume.

Weights and Measures, Property Qualifications and Salaries

Roman coins and measures

aureus ('gold piece')	gold coin (7 g) = 25 *denarii*
denarius ('10 *as* piece')	silver coin (3.5 g) = 4 sesterces
sestertius, sesterce (*HS*)	bronze coin = 2½ asses, used as unit for counting money
as	copper coin
quadrans ('quarter')	copper coin = ¼ *as*
modius	measure of capacity/weight (8.62 l = 6.65 kg wheat)
sextarius ('sixth')	measure of capacity (*c.* 500 ml)
pedalis ('measuring one foot')	29.6 cm
bissales ('measuring two thirds of a foot')	19.7 cm
cubitum ('forearm', cubit)	*c.* 46 cm
milia passuum (mile, Roman, of 'one thousand paces')	*c.* 1479 m
iugerum	square measure (0.25 ha)
centuria	division of land (200 *iugera*)

Greek (Attic) coins and measures, commonly used in Greek-speaking provinces

talent (Attic)	= 6,000 *drachmae*
drachma (Attic)	silver coin (4.36 g) = 6 obols, notionally equivalent to 1 *denarius*. (The Alexandrian drachma used in Egypt was notionally equivalent to one *sestertius*.)
stade	178.6 m
schoenus	measure of distance coverable in one hour, 30–40 stades
plethron	square measure (929 sq. m)

Property Qualifications and Salaries

	HS
To be a Roman senator, a man had to possess property worth at least	1,000,000
The property of the Younger Pliny has been estimated at	20,000,000
He bought one estate (*Ep.* 3.19.7) for	3,000,000
A Roman eques had to possess property worth at least	400,000
A local councillor might have to possess (amounts varied)	100,000
The highest value of the estates of a landowner who borrowed money on the Veleia maintenance schemes (see below, **250**) was	1,200,700
Senators who governed provinces received annual salaries of	400,000
Equites in imperial service would receive salaries of	60,000–200,000
Before Domitian's pay rise, basic legionary annual pay was	900
After the pay rise, it was	1,200
At Rome, men received 60 *modii* of wheat annually, worth	*c.* 300–360

6

Bibliography and Abbreviations

AE — *L'Année épigraphique* (items referred to by year of volume and number of item)

Aphrodisias — J. M. Reynolds, *Aphrodisias and Rome. Documents from the Excavations of the Theatre at Aphrodisias* (1982)

Bar Kokhba Documents — N. Lewis, ed., *The documents from the Bar Kokhba Period in the Cave of Letters. Greek Papyri* (1989)

BMC — *British Museum Catalogue*

CAH — *Cambridge Ancient History*

CPJ — V. Tcherikover, A. Fuks, and M. Stern, *Corpus Papyrorum Judaicarum* (3 vols., 1957–64)

CPL — R. Cavenaile, *Corpus Papyrorum Latinarum* (1958)

CREBM — H. Mattingly *et al.*, *Coins of the Roman Empire in the British Museum* 1 (1923); 2^2 (1978)

EJ^2 — V. Ehrenberg and A. H. M. Jones, *Documents Illustrating the Reigns of Augustus and Tiberius*[2], ed. D. L. Stockton (1976)

Graffites — R. Marichal, *Les Graffites de la Graufesenque. 47e Suppl. à Gallia* (1988)

ILS — H. Dessau, ed., *Inscriptiones Latinae Selectae* (3 vols., 1892–1916, repr. 1954–5)

LACTOR 8 — B. H. Warmington and S. J. Miller, *Inscriptions of the Roman Empire AD 14–117* (LACTOR 8, 1971, repr. 1996)

LACTOR 15 — J. Edmondson, *Dio: the Julio-Claudians: Selections from Books 58–63 of the* Roman History *of Cassius Dio* (LACTOR 15, 1992)

Land-Surveyors — J. B. Campbell, *The Writings of the Roman Land-Surveyors: Text, Translation, and Commentary* (2000)

Ostia — R. Meiggs, *Roman Ostia* (1960, ed. 2 1973)

Military Records — R. O. Fink, *Roman Military Records on Papyrus* (1971)

MW — M. McCrum and A. G. Woodhead, *Select Documents of the Principates of the Flavian Emperors* (1961)

OCD^3 — S. Hornblower and A. Spawforth, edd., *Oxford Classical Dictionary* (ed. 3, 1996)

PMich — *Michigan Papyri* (1931–)

POxy — *Oxyrhynchus Papyri* (1898–)

RIB — R. G. Collingwood and R. P. Wright, edd., *The Roman Inscriptions of Britain*. 1 (1965); S. S. Frere and R. S. Tomlin, 2 (1991)

RIC — H. Mattingly and E. A. Sydenham, *et al.*, edd., *The Roman Imperial Coinage*: 1. *Augustus to Vitellius* (rev. C. H. V. Sutherland, 1984); 2. *Vespasian to Hadrian* (1926)

Sel. Pap.	*Select Papyri*: 2. *Non-literary Papyri; Public Documents* (Loeb Classical Library, 1935)
SC de Cn. Pisone patre	W. Eck *et al.*, edd., *Das senatus consultum de Cn. Pisone patre* (1996)
Sm. *G–N*	E. M. Smallwood, *Documents illustrating the Principates of Gaius, Claudius and Nero* (1967)
Sm. *N–H*	E. M. Smallwood, *Documents illustrating the Principates of Nerva, Trajan and Hadrian* (1966)
Tabula Irnitana	J. González, 'The Lex Irnitana: a new copy of the Flavian Municipal Law', *Journal of Roman Studies* 76 (1986) 147–239
Tabula Siarensis	J. González, *Zeitschift für Papyrologie und Epigraphik* 55 (1984) 55–100; A.Sánchez-Ostiz, *Tabula Siarensis: edición, traducción y comentario* (1999)
Tabulae Pompeianae Sulp.	G. Camodeca, *Tabulae Pompeianae Sulpiciorum (TPSulp): edizione critica dell' archivio puteolano dei Sulpicii* (2 vols., 1999)
Tabulae Vindolandenses II	A. K. Bowman and J. D. Thomas, *The Vindolanda Writing Tablets* (1994)

Editorial Conventions

[ ]	square brackets enclose words or letters which are missing in the original text and have been restored by the editor or translator.
[....]	dots in square brackets represent letters missing in the original text.
[---]	dashes in square brackets represent an uncertain amount of missing text.
( )	round brackets enclose additions to the original text made by the editor or translator, such as the expansion of abbreviated words, or explanatory notes.
< >	angle brackets enclose letters or words omitted by error in the original text.
...	dots outside brackets mark where the translator has omitted part of the text.

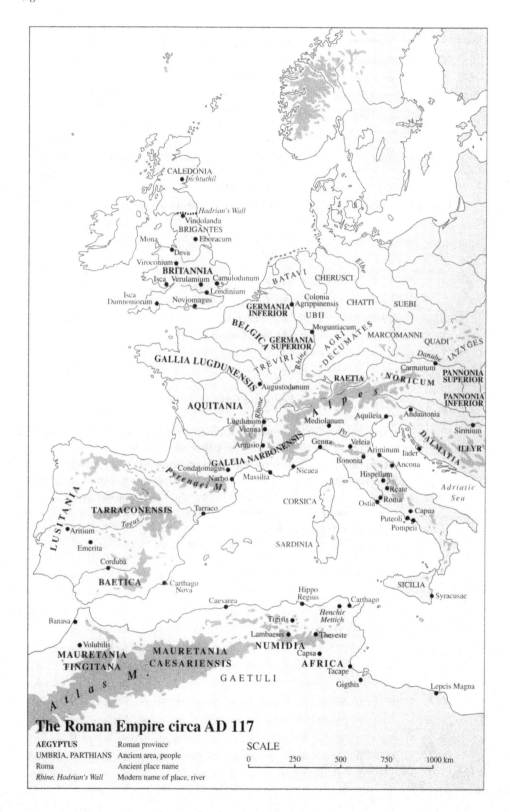

The Roman Empire circa AD 117

		SCALE
AEGYPTUS	Roman province	
UMBRIA, PARTHIANS	Ancient area, people	
Roma	Ancient place name	
Rhine, Hadrian's Wall	Modern name of place, river	

0   250   500   750   1000 km

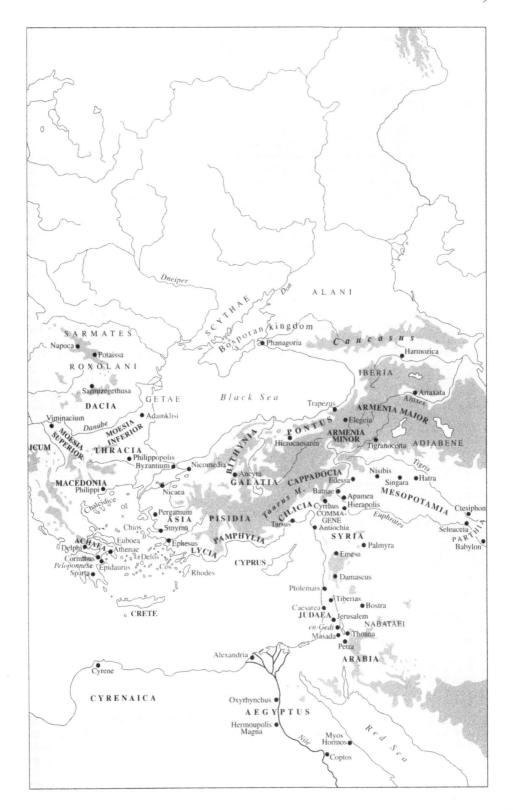

SARMATES
Napoca
Potaissa
ROXOLANI
Sarmizegethusa
DACIA
GETAE
Viminacium
Danube
MOESIA
INFERIOR
ICUM
MOESIA
SUPERIOR
THRACIA
Adamklisi
MACEDONIA
Philippopolis
Philippi
Byzantium
Nicomedia
Nicaea
Chalcidice
Pergamum
ASIA
Chios
Euboea
Smyrna
ACHAEA
Delphi
Athenae
Corinthus
Peloponnese
Sparta
Epidaurus
Delos
Cos
Rhodes
CRETE
Ephesus
LYCIA
PAMPHYLIA
PISIDIA
CYPRUS
CYRENAICA
Cyrene
Alexandria
Oxyrhynchus
AEGYPTUS
Hermoupolis
Magna
Nile
Coptos
Myos
Hormos
Red Sea

Dneiper
Don
SCYTHAE
Bosporan kingdom
Phanagoria
ALANI
Caucasus
Harmozica
IBERIA
Artaxata
Araxes
Black Sea
Trapezus
ARMENIA MAIOR
Elegeia
PONTUS
ARMENIA
MINOR
BITHYNIA
Hierocaesarea
Tigranocerta
ADIABENE
Ancyra
GALATIA
CAPPADOCIA
Tigris
Edessa
Nisibis
Singara
Hatra
Batnae
M.
Taurus
CILICIA
Cyrrhus
Apamea
Hierapolis
MESOPOTAMIA
Ctesiphon
COMMA-
GENE
Tarsus
Antiochia
Euphrates
Seleuceia
PARTHIA
Babylon
SYRIA
Palmyra
Emesa
Damascus
Ptolemais
Tiberias
Bostra
Caesarea
JUDAEA
Jerusalem
NABATAEI
en-Gedi
Masada
Thoana
Petra
ARABIA

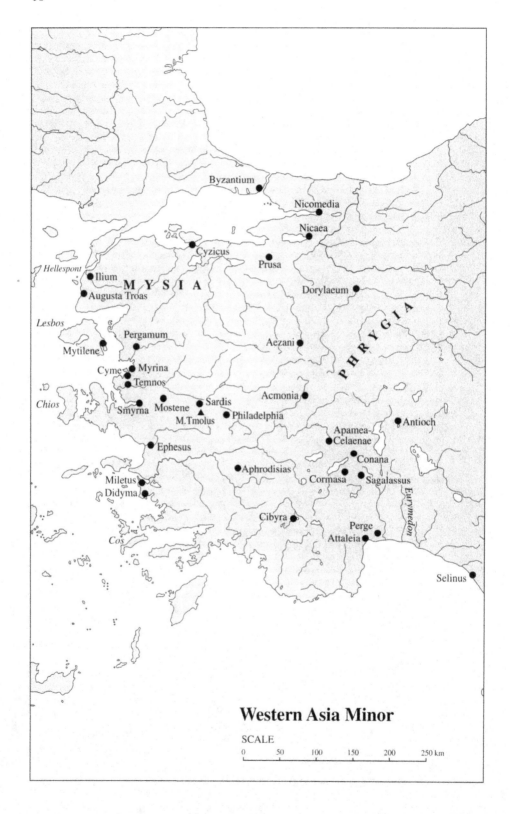

Western Asia Minor

SCALE

| 0 | 50 | 100 | 150 | 200 | 250 km |

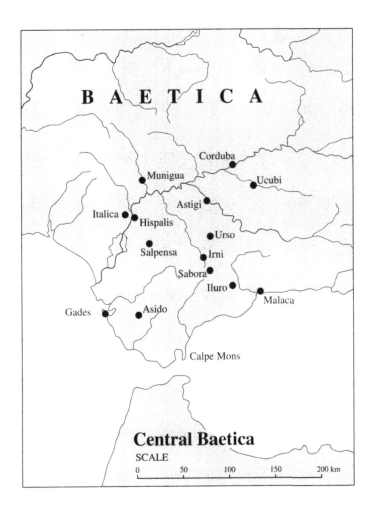

Central Baetica

SCALE

Introduction

The purpose of this volume is to provide sixth-formers and undergraduates, as well as other interested readers, with access to the sources for the period when the Roman Empire developed into its definitive form and approached its apogee (political, economic, military) with the confidence that success encouraged. Recovering under Augustus from the losses and uncertainties of the Civil Wars, the Empire benefited from peace until it was shaken once more in AD 68–9 by the fall of Nero and the Year of the Four Emperors. Those twenty months of instability, which ended when the Flavians established themselves firmly in power, only convinced its inhabitants that the system was indeed durable. Meanwhile, in spite of temporary pauses, the Romans had not given up the idea of potential world conquest. Many smaller acquisitions were eclipsed by the sensational conquest of Britain, even beyond Ocean, and of gold-rich Dacia beyond the Danube. Domestic calm under Trajan was accompanied by Rome's last major imperialistic military success.

The first half of this period is rich in ancient historical writing: above all Tacitus' *Annals*, despite the loss of his account of AD 29–47 and 66–68; for the second half, the three major historical writers fail: Tacitus' *Histories* break off in the autumn of 70, Suetonius' last three biographies are skimpy, and Dio Cassius' work exists only in excerpts and summaries. On the other hand, Pliny's *Letters* are highly informative, and there is a richness of data from inscriptions beyond anything available for earlier periods; confident in the future, people were willing and able to spend more money on setting out their own achievements, and those of their friends, relations and superiors, at greater length then ever before. I have drawn freely upon them, as from papyri and coins.

The material in this volume works on four themes. First comes the controversial topic of aggressive imperialism and its survival into the Empire, and an examination of its development in Europe, Africa and the East. Then the Empire and how it was governed: its structure and the power, actual and potential, of the army. The contentious topic of 'Romanisation' is part of this, and a change of vocabulary is suggested. The realities of power, the vital taxation, the inevitable misgovernment, have to be looked at, with their violent consequence of revolt. Third, there is a section on ideology, 'the imperial cult', and the rôle of the emperors in securing loyalty to Rome. Other religious matters, such as the spread of Christianity and other new cults, developments in philosophy and law, and literary culture, art and entertainment, illustrate the important effect of the provinces on Rome, the last of the four themes, but the economic impact is given greatest weight. Finance through booty and taxation was essential for senate and emperor, both in his official capacity and as the wealthiest politician in the Roman world; if it were not kept on a sound basis disaster was likely to follow, as it did for Nero. The destination of income from booty and taxes is one aspect of this; another was the relative economic success of Italy and the provinces. Italy's traditional status was protected during this period, as shown in taxation privileges, help from the alimentary schemes, freedom from governors, special treatment in Domitian's vine edict, and its contribution to the imperial service (see Section 5.5 below), but was gradually eroded, to Italy's further ultimate disadvantage. Whatever the ultimate outcome for Italy, views of how the Romans acquired their empire, and of their spirit in administering it, have changed over time, from a favourable estimate held during the heyday of the British (and other) empires, to an acceptance after the Second World

War of bare-faced aggression and greed, collective and individual. Very recently in historical and archaeological work a reaction from this unfavourable view can be seen: Rome cared for her subjects, and her rule was accordingly acceptable; and the Empire came about through collaboration between Roman and native élites. Whatever one's view, it is important to beware of accepting half-truths as the whole.

In using the book, readers should remember how closely domestic political issues are intertwined with military, provincial and foreign, even how an emperor's success at Rome depended on his success abroad.

As in other LACTORS, passages from major writers accessible in the Penguin Classics, World's Classics, and other series are given in reference form only: here Tacitus (with one exception), Suetonius, Cassius Dio as far as the items in LACTOR 15 go, and the *Letters* of the younger Pliny). Inscriptions already available in LACTOR 8 are not normally translated here; I have simply given a reference to that publication.

Material is confined to the period AD 14–117, except for a few items that may throw light on that period. All dates are of the Christian era unless otherwise indicated; when Roman datings by consul or emperor's regnal year appear in a text, or a Greek month system, an equivalent has been given as well. All documents are translated from Latin except where indicated. Cross references give readers access to as much diverse material as possible in a book of small compass; items are numbered consecutively throughout.

1. DEVELOPMENTS IN IMPERIALISM

Rome's imperialist drive did not die out under the Principate: maintaining the Empire demanded further profitable conquest, and the emperor himself needed warfare to justify his power and military success to give him more glory than any other commander. Augustus did not just consolidate: he added important provinces to the Empire, such as Egypt and Galatia, and waged aggressive war in Germany from 12 BC until AD 9. Tiberius continued operations in a more cautious way, through diplomacy, while Claudius launched the definitive invasion of Britain (43), taking a conspicuous part himself. When Nero was brought down in 68 he was planning an expedition to the Caucasus in the steps of Pompey the Great. After the civil wars of 68–9, Vespasian restarted the advance west and north in Britain, into Wales and southern Scotland. He also carried through a modest version of Augustus' plans for Germany, occupying lands east of the Rhine. These acquisitions were extended by Domitian along the Danube, and he laid out a whole system of fortifications east of the Rhine.

The Flavians adhered to established imperialist doctrines, as the boundary markers set up at Rome show: they commemorated the fact that Vespasian and Titus, like Claudius, had extended the limits of the Roman Empire, and accordingly those of the city (LACTOR 8, 56). Vespasian built a Temple to Peace (*Pax*), completed in 75, but it was Peace as in 'pacification' (cf. Tacitus, *Agr.* 30.5). About the same time, Pliny was eulogising her.

1   **Pliny, *Natural History* 27.3.**   To think that other plants besides those I have already mentioned are transported from other places, backwards and forwards all over the world for the welfare of the human race, as the boundless majesty of the Roman peace brings into view in turn not only human beings with their different environments and peoples, but also mountains and ranges that reach up into the clouds, the living beings they bring forth, and their plants as well. May that gift of the gods last for ever, I pray! For they seem to have given the Romans as a second source of light for the affairs of human beings.

Domitian's struggles with tribes from north of the Danube and with the Dacians in particular were followed up by Trajan, whose two Dacian wars against King Decebalus (101–2, 104–6) began as an attempt to reduce Decebalus to the status of a dependant and ended with the creation of a new province, Dacia. Trajan was less successful in the East. His annexation of Armenia (114) and attack on the heart of the Parthian territory in Mesopotamia (115–16) was speedy, but ephemeral. As belief in total conquest waned, a suspicion took its place that what was worth acquiring had already been acquired, and, in Britain, more than that: so Appian.

2   **Appian, *Roman History*, *Preface* 5.**   All the islands that are in the Mediterranean … all these are subject to the Romans. And having crossed the northern Ocean to Britain, which is bigger than a large continent, they hold the choicest part of it, more than half, wanting nothing from the rest of it; not even the part they hold is very profitable for them.

2. Imperialism on Three Continents

2.1 Germany

The costly campaigns of 12 BC – AD 6 ended with the defeat of P. Quintilius Varus in 9, but not all the forts in Germany were given up. Germanicus (12–16) staged invasions on a grand scale in his last two years, and clearly intended ultimately to restore Roman rule in German territory between the Rhine and the Elbe. They also were costly, and Germanicus was removed to a command in the East (see Section 2.5 below); his adoptive brother Drusus Caesar must also be given a chance (see Section 2.2 below). (Cf. Tacitus, *Ann.* 1.50–2, 55–71; 2.5–26.)

3   **Dio 57.6.1 and 18.1.**   But Germanicus, afraid even so that the troops would mutiny again, invaded enemy territory and provided them with work there, as well as quantities of supplies from what belonged to others ... [18.1] Germanicus, having acquired a good reputation on the basis of his campaign against the Germans, advanced to the Ocean and decisively defeated the barbarians. He collected up the bones of those who had fallen with Varus and buried them, and recovered the military standards.

Gaius Caligula conducted what may have been exercises in Germany in 39, perhaps following the example of his father Germanicus. Claudius and Nero followed Tiberius' policy of encouraging the German tribes to destroy each other and a commander who in 47 ventured too far into Germany in hot pursuit (Cn. Domitius Corbulo) was told to withdraw (Dio 59.21.3 = LACTOR 15, p. 78; Tacitus, *Ann.* 11.18–19; Suetonius, *Cal.* 45–6).

It was Vespasian who renewed the advance and the 'conquest that was taking so long' (Tacitus, *Germ.* 37.4), aiming at the re-entrant angle between the sources of the Rhine and the Danube, the area called the *Decumates Agri* by Tacitus, *Germ.* 29.3. Roads were built and a town to serve as centre for the area, Arae Flaviae.

4   **MW 416. Milestone, Offenburg. *c.* 73.**   When Caesar [Domitian, son of Augustus,] was consul for the [?third] time and Cn. Cornelius Clemens legate [of Augustus with praetorian rank,] the route was laid down [from] Argentorate to R[aetia] (*or*, to the R[iver Danube's bank])

The triumphal decorations of the general who occupied the area may have been due rather to his rôle in suppressing Civilis' revolt of 69–70 (see Section 3.6 below) than to achievements in the *Decumates Agri*.

5   **MW 50. From Hispellum, Umbria.**   Cn. Pinarius Cornelius [Clemens], son of Lucius, of the Papirian tribe, legate with praetorian rank of the army [stationed in Upper Germany, curator of] sacred [buildings] and public places [---], with triumphal decorations [on account of successes] in Germany

Domitian was active further north on the Rhine, defeating the Chatti in 83, and establishing a frontier marked by a wooden palisade, along the Wetterau east of the

Rhine. This was a permanent achievement, although the reports of senatorial historians hostile to the emperor are unfavourable.

6 **Dio 67.3.5 – 4.1.** And after this (trial of the Vestals, *c*. 83) he set out for Gaul and plundered some of the peoples beyond the Rhine who enjoyed treaties with Rome. He became as puffed up as if he had put something important to rights and he increased the soldiers' pay, perhaps on account of the victory; each man had been receiving 75 drachmas, and he ordered them to be given 100. When he came to regret this, he did not decrease the amount, but cut down the number of soldiers. On both accounts the damage he did to the state was considerable: he made the numbers of men defending it inadequate and those that it did have costly to pay for. [4.1] He made a foray into Germany and returned without even having caught a glimpse of warfare. Why should I go on to talk about the honours that were conferred both on him at that time and on occasion on other emperors similar to him with the idea of preventing them from suspecting from the paucity and insignificance of the honours that they had been seen through, and so getting angry?

In about 90 the Cherusci had to acknowledge the change in their position, and the Romans accepted the fact that their Cheruscan puppet ruler could not command adequate support in the tribe.

7 **Dio 67.5.1.** Chariomerus, king of the Cherusci, had been driven out of his kingdom by the Chatti because of his friendship with the Romans. At first he enlisted the help of some others and made a successful return, but later, when he sent hostages to the Romans, they deserted him. He threw himself on Domitian's mercy, and although he received no military backup, he was given financial support.

Domitian's advance is marked on the coinage.

8 **MW 57. *Sestertius*. 85.** *Obverse*. Bust of Domitian, laureate, bearded, with aegis. EMPEROR CAESAR DOMITIAN AUGUSTUS GERMANICUS ELEVEN TIMES CONSUL.
   Reverse. German, standing in front of trophy, hands tied behind back; German woman seated, mourning. GERMANY ANNEXED. BY DECREE OF THE SENATE.

Domitian was not totally successful: the Chatti were still involved in the revolt of Antonius Saturninus, commander of the Upper Rhine army, in January 89, when they were prevented from helping him only by a thawing of the river (Suetonius, *Dom.* 6.2). The revolt was put down by the commander of the Lower Rhine army, A. Lappius Maximus, and a campaign against the Chatti followed, for which Domitian celebrated a triumph (LACTOR 8, 71). It was a 'German War'.

9 **MW 60. Rome.** To [---]elia, wife of [L]appius Maximus, who brought the German War to an end.

In 97 Nerva received the title Germanicus for Trajan's success in Germany (LACTOR 8, 76(e) and (f)), but danger in this area was diminished by continuing strife between the tribes (Tacitus, *Germ.* 33).

Under the Flavians, after 77 when Pliny published the *Natural Histories*, the military commands of the Upper and Lower Rhine armies became regular provincial governorships of the two military zones.

2.2 The Danube

There was no sharp distinction between the Rhine and Danube spheres of operation: Tacitus' *Germania* deals with tribes beyond both rivers, but Roman territory south of the Danube was particularly threatened by tribes living beyond it and by Roxolani ('Red Alans'), immigrants from the steppes of Asia who had other tribes behind them. Then there were the well-organised Dacians under King Decebalus, who had already been considered a serious threat in Caesar's time. The power of this kingdom was due to its wealth in gold, which also made it an attractive target.

The increasing importance of the Danube from Augustus to Trajan during this period is shown by the build-up of legions and auxiliary forces, and by the splitting into two provinces of Moesia in the mid-eighties.

10   **MW 307. From Andautonia, Pannonia.**   To Lucius Funisulanus Vettonianus, son of Lucius, of the Aniensis tribe, military tribune of the Sixth, Victorious, Legion, quaestor of the province of Sicily, tribune of the plebs, praetor, legate of the Fourth, Scythian, Legion, prefect of the Aerarium of Saturn, curator of the Aemilian Road, consul, member of the seven-man college of priests in charge of banquets, legate of praetorian rank of the province of Dalmatia, likewise of the province of Pannonia, and of Upper Moesia, awarded [by Emperor Domitian Augustus Germanicus] in the Dacian War four crowns, mural, rampart, naval and golden, four untipped spears, four banners. By decree of the city council, to its patron.

Pannonia was also divided after the Dacian War, 106: Sm. *N–H* 352 is a military discharge certificate of 19 November 102, that mentions units 'in Pannonia under Q. Glitius Agricola', while the future Emperor Hadrian governed part of the divided province.

11   *Historia Augusta, Hadrian* **3.8–10.**   (Hadrian) became praetor … [9] Afterwards he was sent as legate with praetorian rank to Lower Pannonia. He brought the Sarmatians under control, maintained discipline among the soldiers, and checked the procurators, who were straying too far from the proper path. [10] Consequently he was made consul (108).

Splitting provinces helped deal with the length of the frontier along the Danube and the multiplicity of potential opponents.

Already from 17 to 20 Drusus Caesar held a special commission in the Balkans, supervising the existing provinces, Dalmatia and Pannonia (if they were already separated), and probably Moesia as well. Drusus helped bring about the fall of the formidable King Maroboduus of the Marcomanni and eventually placed the remains of the kingdom in the hands of the Quadian Vannius (Tacitus, *Ann.* 2.44–6; 3.7; 10). Drusus' officers also dealt with pirates operating in the Dardanelles.

12 EJ² 227. Ilium, Asia. Greek. The council and people honoured Titus Valerius Proculus, procurator of Drusus Caesar, who destroyed the pirate vessels in the Hellespont and kept the city in every respect free of burdens.

In 50 Vannius was expelled by his nephews Vangio and Sido, and Claudius ordered a watch on the Danube (Tacitus, *Ann.* 12.29–30). Unrest in the reign of Nero was met by an energetic response from the governor of Moesia, Tiberius Plautius Aelianus Silvanus (LACTOR 8, 42). Hostile incursions over the Danube began in the winter of 67–8: the Roxolani, now in Wallachia, had cut up two auxiliary cohorts, but in February 69 an expedition of up to 9,000 tribesmen was destroyed by the Third, Gallica, Legion and auxiliary troops (Tacitus, *Hist.* 1.79.1–4.). But the Flavian leadership withdrew troops and in late September 69 the Dacians moved against Oescus and Novae. Mucianus' task-force, en route for Italy, turned north, and the Sixth, Ferrata, Legion went to repel the Dacians (Tacitus, *Hist.* 3.46). In late autumn, C. Fonteius Agrippa was brought up from Asia with additional forces, to co-ordinate defence. (Cf. Section 3.6 below for the rebellion Josephus mentions.)

13 Josephus, *Jewish War* **7.89–95.** At the very same time as the revolt of the Germans that I have described there coincided a bold attack on the Romans made by the Scythians. [90] For the section of the Scythians called the Sarmatians, who are very numerous, crossed the Danube to the Roman side without being noticed. The incursion was very violent and they were hard to deal with because their arrival was totally unexpected. They massacred large numbers of the Romans on guard, [91] including the legate and ex-consul Fonteius Agrippa who came up to meet them, and whom they killed fighting valiantly. They overran the whole adjacent country, plundering and pillaging whatever they fell on. [92] Vespasian heard what had happened and of the devastation of Moesia and sent Rubrius Gallus to bring the Sarmatians to justice. [93] At his hands numbers of them fell in the fighting and the remnant fled in terror to their own territory. [94] The general, having put an end to the war in this way, took thought for future security. He distributed larger garrisons in the area and at more frequent intervals, so as to make the crossing completely impossible for the barbarians. [95] The war in Moesia, then, reached a quick resolution in this way.

At the north-eastern extremity of Roman dominions, Vespasian had reaffirmed the Roman protectorate in the Bosporan kingdom; Rhescuporis ruled from 77 to 96.

14 MW 233. Phanagoria, Crimean Bosporus. Greek. Emperor Vespasian Caesar [Augustus, Supreme Pontiff, hailed Imperator] for the sixth time, Father of the Fatherland, [three times consul, designated consul for the fourth time], lord of the entire Bosporus [---] piously, justly, of the hereditary king Tiberius Claudius Rhescuporis, son of King Julius [---], friend of Caesar, friend of the Romans, High Priest of the Augusti for life, and benefactor of his fatherland [---]

15   **MW 236. Bosporus.** *Aureus* **of 87.**   *Obverse.* Bust of Rhescuporis II, wearing diadem. TIBERIUS JULIUS KING RHESCUPORIS.
    Reverse. Head of Domitian, laureate. 384 (year of the Bosporan era)

On the Danube, Domitian continued Vespasian's advance north of the river. Flavian defensive measures were adequate until the early eighties. The sixth-century monk Jordanes summarised activities in his history of his people.

16   **Jordanes,** *Getica* **12–13.**   This country within sight of Moesia on the far side of the Danube is surrounded by a ring of mountains. It has only two routes into it, one by Boutae, the other by Tapae … [13] For after a long interval, when Emperor Domitian was on the throne and they feared his greed, the Goths broke the treaty that they had long since struck with other emperors. They laid waste the Danube bank, which had long been in possession of the Romans, crushing the troops along with their generals. Oppius Sabinus was governing the province at that time, after Agrippa, while the Goths were under the rule of Dorpaneus. The Goths embarked on the war, defeated the Romans, cut off the head of Sabinus, took over numerous forts and settlement, openly plundering what belonged to the emperor. This was a crisis for his people, and Domitian hastened with all his forces into Illyricum, with soldiers drawn from almost the entire state. Fuscus as general was sent on ahead, along with the cream of the soldiery, and making a pontoon bridge of boats he forced them to cross the River Danube beyond the army of Dorpaneus. Then the Dacians, proving no slouches, took up their weapons, and, armed as they were, in the first encounter lost no time in defeating the Romans. The commander Fuscus was killed, and they stripped the camp of the solders' valuables. Having won an important victory in the region, they now began to call their leading warriors, as men who had won their victory with fortune's favour, not simple men, but demigods – 'Anses' in their language.

There was a Dacian incursion into Moesia in the winter of 84–5. It was met by the governor Oppius Sabinus, but he was killed (Suetonius, *Dom.* 6.1). Domitian was summoned from his activities on the Rhine to meet the challenge in 85 and organise reprisals; he never returned to Germany; but his use of Cornelius Fuscus, Prefect of the Praetorian Guard, as commander against the Dacians proved disastrous.

17   **Dio 67.6.1, 3–5.**   The Romans had a very serious war on their hands with the Dacians, whose king at that time was Decebalus. He was formidable in the theory and practice of warfare, good at choosing the moment to attack and equally opportune in retreat, a skilled hand at ambushes and effective in pitched battles; he knew how to follow up a victory well and how to manage a reverse. This certainly made him a worthy opponent of the Romans over a long period … [6.3] So Domitian made an expedition against them; not that he took personal control of the war, but stayed in a city in Moesia, behaving in his usual outrageous way … [6.4] He sent other commanders to the war, more often with bad results.
    [6.5] Decebalus, king of the Dacians, was sending envoys to Domitian with promises of peace. But Domitian sent Fuscus against him with a large force. When Decebalus heard of this he sent another embassy to him with the idea of scoffing at him. The proposal was to make peace with Domitian on condition that

every Roman should opt to pay Decebalus a tribute of two obols *per annum*; if he did not, Decebalus would make war on them and inflict huge misfortunes on them.

An attack on the capital Sarmizegethusa had to be put off and a peace patched up: the Quadi and Marcomanni were causing trouble again in 89, perhaps provoked by Roman activities.

18 Dio 67.7.1–4. Domitian wanted to pay out the Quadi and Marcomanni because they had not helped him against the Dacians. He entered Pannonia to make war on them, and killed the second set of envoys who had been sent to talk peace.
[7.2] Domitian, defeated by the Marcomanni and taking to flight, lost no time in sending to Decebalus king of the Dacians, and induced him to make a truce which he had formerly refused Decebalus when he frequently requested it. Decebalus accepted the truce: he had been through extreme hardships. All the same, Domitian was not willing to negotiate with Decebalus face to face, but sent Diegis with some men to present Decebalus with weapons and some prisoners, allegedly the only ones he had. [7.3] When this had been done, Domitian put a diadem on the head of Diegis as if he had won a real victory and was in a position to bestow any king on the Dacians; and to the soldiers he gave awards and money. And among the other things he sent to Rome, as if he had won a victory, were envoys from Decebalus and what he claimed was a letter from Decebalus, which he was said to have forged. [7.4] He used a good deal of triumphal furniture to make the festival finer, objects that were not selected from items he had captured. Quite the reverse: he had actually spent extra on the truce, giving quantities of money to Decebalus on the spot, and workers skilled at every trade whether of war or peace, and promising to go on giving quantities in perpetuity. The items on display came from the imperial furniture.

19 MW 140. Puteoli. 86. To Emperor Caesar Domitian Augustus Germanicus, son of the deified Vespasian, Supreme Pontiff, in his [sixth] year of tribunician power, hailed Imperator for the thirteenth time, consul twelve times, censor for an unlimited period, Father of the Fatherland, the Flavian Augustan Colony of Puteoli, through the condescension of the greatest and divine Princeps, the Dacian victory, to [-] (*The whole inscription had been erased.*)

The Roman defeat at the hands of the Dacians was avenged by Tettius Julianus in 88.

20 Dio 67.10.1–3. These things also worth noting happened in the Dacian War. Julianus, who had been put in charge of the war by the Emperor, prepared for it well in a number of ways, including ordering the soldiers to write their own names and those of their centurions on their shields, to make any of them who did anything particularly good or bad more easily recognisable. [10.2] He encountered the enemy at Tapae and slaughtered a very large number of them. Lying among the enemy dead was Vezinas, Decebalus' second-in-command, who, since he could not get away alive, collapsed deliberately, pretending to be dead already, and consequently got away unseen. [10.3] Decebalus, then, afraid that the Romans would exploit their victory to make for the royal headquarters, felled the trees on the site and dressed the stumps in armour, so that the Romans might mistake them for soldiers, take fright, and withdraw; which was just what happened.

War broke out again in 92 with the Sarmatians and Suebi, who had united.

21   Dio 67.5.2.   In Moesia the Lygians, who had been at war with the Suebi, sent envoys asking for an alliance from Domitian, and obtained one that was not strong in numbers, but was distinguished: for only one hundred cavalrymen were given them. The Suebi took offence at this, united some Iazyges with themselves, and began preparations to cross the Danube with them.

Domitian himself went to the scene and detachments of nine legions took part under the equestrian C. Velius Rufus (LACTOR 8, 79). But this was the war in which the Twenty-first, Rapax, Legion was lost; Domitian celebrated only an ovation. The high cost of these wars is shown by the altar erected to the memory of *c.* 3,000 killed.

22   *ILS* 9107. Adamklisi.
[In ...] memory of the most valiant [men]
[who ...] met their death in defence of the Republic

The fragments reveal the names of Romans from Italy (the commanding officer from Pompeii), Narbonensian Gaul, the Rhineland, and Noricum; many peregrine names, belonging to auxiliary troops, are mentioned.
Domitian also undertook engineering works.

23   MW 420. By the cataracts of the Lower Danube, near Taliata in Upper Moesia. 92–3.   Emperor Caesar [Domitian] Augustus Germanicus, son of the deified Vespasian, Supreme Pontiff, in his twenty-second year of tribunician power, consul for the sixteenth time, censor for an unlimited period, Father of the Fatherland, by means of [new] works from Taliata re[made and extended] the route along the Scrofulae [-], which had been eroded by age and the floods from the Danube. The Seventh, Claudian, Legion, devoted and loyal.

German and Sarmatian wars in the reigns preceding Trajan's were the basis of many a distinguished military career.

24   Sm. *N–H* 297. Tifernum Mataurense, Umbria.   To Lucius Aconius Statura, son of Lucius, of the Clustumina tribe, centurion of the Eleventh, Claudian, Legion, devoted and loyal, of the Fourth, Flavian, Legion, the firm, of the Fifth, Macedonian, Legion, of the Seventh, Claudian, Legion, devoted and loyal; awarded decorations by Emperor Trajan Augustus Germanicus for the Dacian War, twisted necklets, armbands, and chest-plates, the rampart crown; and by earlier leaders awarded the same decorations for the German and Sarmatian war; transferred by the deified Trajan from his military service to the rank of eques; quinquennial magistrate and pontiff at Ariminum; quinquennial magistrate, flamen, and pontiff at Tifernum Mataurense. Lucius Aconius Statura, his son, in accordance with his will. At the dedication of the monument he provided a banquet for the members of the city council and the commons. Place for the inscription provided by decree of the council.

There were still large forces at Viminacium, Moesia, at the time of Domitian's death, presaging future warfare. Either in 97 or in 101, just before Trajan's first Dacian War, they were visited by a sophist and philosopher, who reported it in his speech at the Olympic Games, referring to the Moesians as identical with the Mysians of north-west Asia Minor, and quoting Homer's *Iliad* 21.50.

25 Dio of Prusa 12.16–19. As a matter of fact, I happen at this moment to have been on a long journey, right to the Danube and the land of the Getae or Mysians, as Homer says, following the current name of the people. |17| I journeyed, not as a merchant travelling in goods for sale, and not in army service as a baggage carrier or cattle driver, nor yet was I on an embassy connected with our allies, or on a complimentary mission of men whose united prayers are no more than lip-service; I,
    One stripped of weapons, helmet, shield, and spear,
had no other weapon either. [18] So that I was surprised how they could put up with the sight of me: I had no knowledge of horsemanship, was useless as an archer or infantryman, nor was I a lancer or slinger belonging to the light-armed soldiers who do not have to carry heavy weaponry; nor was I able to cut wood or dig a ditch, or cut fodder from the enemy's fields – with many a glance over my shoulder! – nor could I put up a tent or a rampart as some helpers do who, helpless as they are, still follow the legions. |19| As far as all this was concerned I was helpless, and arrived among men who were not stupid and yet had no time to listen to speeches. They were wound up and anxious like race-horses at the starting gate, unable to put up with the waiting, pitting the ground with their hooves in their eagerness and excitement. There you could see swords everywhere, breastplates everywhere, spears everywhere; everything was full of horses, weapons, armed men.

Back on the Danube, Trajan prepared for his war against the Dacians by engineering works designed to facilitate transport.

26 Sm. *N–H* 413, cut in the cliff on the right bank of the Danube west of Orsava, Upper Moesia. 100. Emperor Caesar Nerva Trajan Augustus Germanicus, son of the deified Nerva, Supreme Pontiff, in his fourth year of tribunician power, Father of the Fatherland, holder of the consulship for the third time, cut open the mountainsides, removed the projecting elbows of rock, and built a road.

Trajan's operations at the Iron Gate were designed to help shipping on the river.

27 J.Šašel, *Journal of Roman Studies* 63 (1973) 80–5: marble slab from Karataš. 101. Emperor Nerva Trajan Augustus Germanicus, son of the deified Nerva, Supreme Pontiff, in his fifth year of tribunician power, Father of the Fatherland, four times consul, diverted the river on account of the danger caused by the cataracts, and made the Danube safe for navigation.

Trajan set out on 25 March 101, and the Arval Brethren took a vow for his safe return and victory.

28   Sm. *N–H*, pp. 14–15.   When Quintus Articuleius [Paetus] and Sextus Attius Suburanus were consuls, on the eighth day before the Kalends of April, on the Capitol [for the safety and return] and victory of Emperor Caesar Nerva Trajan Augustus Germanicus the Arval [Brethren took vows] in these words which are written below: Jupiter Best and Greatest, we pray to you and implore you and call you to witness, that you make Emperor Caesar Nerva Trajan Augustus Germanicus, son of the Deified Nerva, our leader and parent, holder of the supreme pontificate and of tribunician power, Father of the Fatherland, him of whom we are aware [of speaking], return well and in good fortune, [unharmed] and victorious from those regions and provinces, and that you grant [a happy outcome] to him of those affairs which he is now transacting and [is] about to transact, and that you preserve him in that condition in which he now is or in a better one, and that you place [him returned], unharmed and victorious in the city of Rome at the first possible time. [And if you shall perform those things in that manner], we vow that there [shall be] a sacrifice of an ox with gilded horns in the name of the college of Arval Brethren.

Engineering works on campaign in Dacia, probably with Trajan in 101, are described in Balbus' work on land-surveying, *The Description and Analysis of All Shapes*, addressed to Celsus.

29   *Land-Surveyors* 204–5, with diagrams (92–3 Lachmann).   The brilliant expedition of our most sacred Emperor interrupted me and lured me away, for all my speed in writing. For, while I gave more attention to warfare, I gave up this whole occupation, practically forgetting it, and thought of nothing but the glory of war. But as soon as we first entered enemy territory, the works of our Emperor began to demand the calculation of measurements. Two straight lines in a certain direction had to be laid down with a fixed space between for the roadway. These were to be the means of producing a vast earthwork that was to rise to protect communications. These lines were revealed by using the iron-based surveying instrument, when part of the work had been brought into the line of vision. As to gauging the dimensions of bridges, we were able to state the width of the river from the nearest bank even if the enemy were intent on harassing us. Calculation, which is revered by the gods, was showing us how to work out the heights of mountains that had to be stormed. After she had been tested in events of great importance, in which I played a part, I began to put her in all shrines as an object of worship and to venerate and cultivate her with greater reverence, and I hastened to complete this book as if I were fulfilling a vow. Therefore, after our greatest Emperor had very recently opened up Dacia with his victory, and immediately granted permission for me to leave that northern region on a year's leave, I returned to my pursuit as if I were going on holiday.

Dio tells the outcome.

30   Dio 68.6.1–2; 8.1 – 9.7; 10.2.   Having spent some time in Rome, he (Trajan) campaigned against the Dacians. He was reckoning up what they had done and resented the sums of money that they were taking every year; he observed that their forces were increasing, and their arrogance. [6.2] When Decebalus heard of his setting out he took fright; he knew perfectly well that previously it was not the Romans but Domitian that he had beaten; now it was the Romans, and Trajan, that he would be fighting ... [8.1] For these reasons (Trajan's merits) it was reasonable for Decebalus to be afraid. When Trajan was on campaign against the Dacians and was approaching Tapae, where the barbarians had their camp, a great mushroom was brought to him, bearing a message in Latin letters that the Buri as well as other allies recommended Trajan to beat a retreat and keep the peace. [8.2] In spite of that Trajan went into battle and saw many of his own men wounded, while he killed a large number of the enemy. And when there was a shortage of dressings, he is said not to have spared his own clothes, but to have cut them into bandages. As for the soldiers killed in the battle, he ordered an altar to be set up and an annual service of commemoration. [9.1] Decebalus had sent envoys even before his defeat, not as before men who had allowed their hair to grow, but the most distinguished of those who wear the cap. [9.2] These men who threw down their weapons and prostrated themselves on the ground asked Trajan preferably to allow Decebalus to meet him face to face and confer with him; he would do everything that was required of him. Failing that, someone else should at least be sent to make terms with him. The men who were sent were Sura and Claudius Livianus, the guard prefect. [9.3] Nothing was achieved, because Decebalus did not dare to deal with them either, sending to them on this occasion also. Trajan took some fortified mountains, and on them found the captured war machines, and the standard taken at the time of Fuscus. [9.4] For this reason, and because Maximus had at the same time captured his sister and a stronghold, Decebalus held himself ready to accept the demands without exception. Not that he intended to keep to them, but to get breathing space in his present situation. [9.5] For he reluctantly agreed to surrender the weapons, war machines and engineers and to return the deserters, to pull down his forts and withdraw from conquered territory, and further to deem the same people as the Romans enemies and friends, and not to accept any deserter nor to employ any soldier from the Roman Empire (for he was recruiting the great majority of his men, and the pick of them, by winning over recruits from there) ... [9.7] ... Trajan made this agreement, left the camp at Sarmizegethusa, and distributed garrisons round the rest of the country. He then returned to Italy ... [10.2] Trajan celebrated a triumph, and was given the title 'Dacicus'.

But Decebalus made a pre-emptive strike on the newly annexed territory of Banat. Trajan had to increase his massive forces, now with the intention of ending the kingdom: he created two new legions, the Second, Trajanic Courageous and the Thirtieth, Ulpian Victorious, and Trajan's Column in Rome, erected to commemorate his campaigns, and prime evidence for them, shows his negotiations with potential allies, German tribes and Greeks from the Black Sea cities.

31 **Dio 68.10.3 – 11.3; 13.1–2, 5–6; 14.1, 3–4; 15.1.** But when Decebalus was being reported to Trajan as acting contrary to the treaty in many ways – he was preparing weapons, receiving those who were deserting, repairing the forts, sending envoys to his neighbours, and harassing those who had previously been on bad terms with him, and he annexed some territory of the Iazyges (which Trajan later did not return to them when they asked for it) – [10.4] the senate accordingly voted him an enemy once again and Trajan as before made war against him in person rather than performing the functions of general by proxy. [11.1] The Dacians were going over to Trajan in droves, so Decebalus, for this as well as other reasons, asked for peace. But he could not be induced to surrender his weapons and himself, and began to mass his forces openly and rally the surrounding tribes: [11.2] if they gave him up they would be in danger themselves; it was safer and easier to fight alongside him in defence of their freedom before they came to any harm, rather than ignore the destruction of his men and get the worst of it later, when they had been stripped of allies. [11.3] Decebalus was doing badly in open battle, but nearly brought about Trajan's death by trickery and deceit. He sent some deserters into Moesia to see if they could do away with him, because, while Trajan was approachable at other times, under pressure of the war he was then admitting to discussions absolutely anyone who wanted. But they were unable to achieve it, because one of them aroused suspicion and was arrested, and under torture admitted Decebalus' entire plot.

[13.1] Trajan built a stone bridge over the Danube, for which I am at a lost to praise him enough. His other achievements are extremely distinguished, but this goes beyond them. It has twenty piers of squared masonry which are 150 feet in height, not counting the foundations, and 60 feet in width; [13.2] these are 170 feet apart and are united by a construction of arches. How could one fail, then, to marvel at the cost that was met for them? Or at the way each part of them came to be in a deep river, full of eddies, on a muddy bottom? For it was impossible, you understand, to divert the stream anywhere else ... [13.5] This also, then, shows Trajan's grand way of thinking; not however that the bridge affords us any advantage: only the piers are standing, and offer no means of crossing. It is as if they had come into being for this purpose alone: that of demonstrating human nature's ability to achieve anything. [13.6] Trajan was afraid that one day the Danube might freeze and war be waged against the Romans on the far bank, and he made the bridge to provide easy access to those crossing over. But Hadrian had the opposite fear, that the barbarians might have an easier crossing into Moesia once they had forced the guard on the bridge, and he removed the superstructure. [14.1] Trajan crossed the Danube by means of this bridge and campaigned in a cautious rather than an energetic way, and after some time with difficulty subdued the Dacians. He presented many examples of generalship and courage, and his troops ran many risks and showed great gallantry for him ... [14.3] Decebalus, when even his royal stronghold and his entire country was captured and he was himself in danger of being taken, made away with himself, and his head was brought to Rome. And so Dacia became subject to the Romans, and Trajan founded cities in it. [14.4] The treasures of Decebalus were also discovered, although they were hidden under the river Sargetia which ran by his royal stronghold ... [15.1] When Trajan had returned to Rome, very large numbers of embassies came to him from the Indians, as well as other barbarians.

A famous inscription commemorates the soldier who found Decebalus' body.

32   M. Speidel, 'The captor of Decebalus, a new inscription from Philippi', *Journal of Roman Studies* **60 (1970) 142–53 (photograph).**   Tiberius Claudius Maximus, veteran, had the monument set up in his own lifetime. He served as a cavalryman in the Seventh, Claudian, Legion, devoted and loyal, was made treasurer of legionary cavalry, personal bodyguard of the legate of the same legion, standard-bearer of the legionary cavalry, sent on cavalry detachment, likewise decorated for valour in the Dacian War by Emperor Domitian; made officer on double rations by the deified Trajan in the second cavalry squadron of Pannonians; by whom he was also made scout in the Dacian War and was twice decorated for valour in the Dacian War and once in the Parthian War; and by the same was made decurion in the same squadron, because he took Decebalus and conveyed his head to Trajan at Ranisstorum. He was granted honourable discharge as a volunteer serving beyond the required term by Terentius Scaurianus, consular governor of the army of the new province [of Mesopotamia?]

The fate of Decebalus' head at Rome is recorded in a fragment of the Calendar of Ostia for 106.

33 Sm. *N–H* 20. [---] of Decebalus [--- ?lay on] on the Gemonian Steps [--- Emperor Nerva Trajan Caesar] Augustus Germanicus Dacicus [---]

Trajan set up a great cenotaph to his success and to Mars the Avenger, the *Tropaeum Traiani* (LACTOR 8, 88) near the memorial commemorating those killed in Domitian's time. Triumphal honours were allowed generals such as Sosius Senecio (LACTOR 8, 86(a) and 87), but the career of an eques who distinguished himself in the war was evidently speeded up because of it; he was governor of Thrace before 106. (See also Section 3.1 below.)

34 Sm. *N–H* 277. Reate, Sabine territory, Italy. To [Publius] Prifernius Paetus Memmius Apollinaris, son of Publius, of the Quirina tribe; member of the quinquennial board of four with jurisdiction; master of the youth; prefect of the Third Cohort of Breucians; military tribune of the Tenth, Gemina, Legion; prefect of the First squadron of Asturians; awarded the untipped lance, banner and mural crown by the Emperor Trajan on the Dacian campaign; procurator of the province of Sicily; procurator of the province of Lusitania; procurator of the five per cent inheritance tax; procurator of the province of Thrace; procurator of the province of Noricum; set up by Publius Memmius Apollinaris, son of Publius, of the Quirina tribe, to his devoted father.

The career of Ti. Claudius Vitalis illustrates the effect that high social standing, as well as the mere gallantry of Ti. Claudius Maximus, could have, as well as the pull that the Danube was having on Rome's stretched military resources: Vitalis served first in Lower Moesia; the First, Minervian, Legion left Lower Germany for the Danube in 101–2; he then served with two legions in Britain but returned to Upper Moesia for his final posting.

35 Sm. *N–H* 294. Rome. Dedicated to Tiberius Claudius Vitalis, son of Tiberius, of the Galerian tribe; he gave up the rank of Roman eques and accepted a centurionate in the Fifth, Macedonian, Legion; was advanced from the Fifth, Macedonian, Legion, to the [First], Italian, Legion; was awarded the twisted necklet, armbands, chestpiece and rampart crown in the Dacian War; was advanced from the First, Italian, Legion, to the First, Minervian; was again awarded the twisted necklet (etc.), in the Dacian War; was advanced from the First, Minervian, Legion, to the Twentieth, Victorious; was likewise promoted in the same legion and further advanced from the Twentieth, Victorious, Legion, to the Ninth, Hispanic; was advanced from the Ninth, Hispanic, Legion, to the Seventh, loyal and faithful; was further advanced in the same legion, served in the second cohort as the fourth ranking centurion for seven years; lived to the age of 41.

Dacia became a province under a governor of consular rank with a garrison of one legion, strengthened by the settlement of a veteran colony with the same name as Decebalus' old capital, Sarmizegethusa (LACTOR 8, 85). Some time between 103 and 111 the Danube was shown reclining on Trajan's coin reverses (LACTOR 8, 84). The coins now celebrated more than 'the defeat of Dacia'.

36   Sm. *N–H* 34(b). *Denarius* struck at Rome.   *Obverse.* Bust of Trajan, laureate. TO EMPEROR TRAJAN AUGUSTUS GERMANICUS DACICUS, SUPREME PONTIFF, HOLDER OF THE TRIBUNICIAN POWER.
   Reverse. A Dacian standing with his hands bound beside a pile of arms. CONSUL FIVE TIMES, FATHER OF THE FATHERLAND, THE SENATE AND ROMAN PEOPLE. ON DACIA'S ANNEXATION.

2.3 Britain

When the reign of Tiberius opened the Romans had given up the idea of turning Julius Caesar's two expeditions (the second of 54 BC a serious attempt to impose Roman control), into a permanent conquest. Augustus simply kept the tribes closest to the Channel coast amenable, and recognised one ruler after another, no matter how they came to power, provided that they acknowledged Rome's overlordship.
   After 10, Cunobelin ('Cymbeline'), king of the Catuvellauni centring on Hertfordshire, brought the Trinobantes of Essex into alliance. His son Adminius, who ruled in Kent, fell out with him and was expelled. He fled to Gaius Caligula and was received as if that meant the accession of all Britain to the Empire (Suetonius, *Cal.* 44.2).
   Gaius did nothing serious towards invading (Suetonius, *Cal.* 46; Dio 59.25.1–3 = LACTOR 15, p. 80), but on Cunobelin's death two other sons, Togodumnus and Caratacus ('Caractacus'), took over and failed to show Rome respect. Claudius needed to prove himself as a soldier. The preparations were meticulous, and in 43 three legions under Aulus Plautius, previously governor of Pannonia, began the conquest, landing either at Richborough or, as has also been argued, near the later palace of Fishbourne in Sussex. When the general claimed to need imperial help, Claudius advanced with a train of elephants and proceeded towards Camulodunum, where a council of chieftains ready to swear allegiance was assembled. In the south and west of the country the later emperor Vespasian with the Second Legion captured the Isle of Wight and reached the site of Exeter (Suetonius, *Claud.* 17; *Vesp.* 4.2–3; Dio 60.19–23 = LACTOR 15, pp. 96–9). The success was celebrated on coins.

37 **Sm.** *G–N* **43(a).** *Aureus.* **Rome. 46–7.** *Obverse.* Head of Claudius, laureate. TIBERIUS CLAUDIUS CAESAR AUGUSTUS, SUPREME PONTIFF, IN HIS SIXTH YEAR OF TRIBUNICIAN POWER, HAILED IMPERATOR TEN TIMES.

Reverse. Triumphal arch surmounted by an equestrian statue between two trophies; on the architrave OVER THE BRITONS.

The triumphal arch theme was taken up in provinces.

38 **Sm.** *G–N* **45. Cyzicus, Asia, on a triumphal arch. ?51–2.** To the deified Augustus Caesar; to Tiberius Augustus [son of the deified Augustus] Emperor; to Tiberius Claudius [Caesar Augustus] Germanicus, Supreme Pontiff, [in his eleventh year of tribunician power, five times consul, having been saluted Imperator ?22 times], Father of the Fatherland, champion of freedom, conqueror [of eleven kings] of Britain, the Roman citizens who reside in Cyzicus and the Cyzicenes set up the arch, under the supervision of [---]

The onslaught continued under another tried commander, Publius Ostorius Scapula (47–51), but after his death during a failed attack on south Wales, Aulus Didius Gallus was sent to consolidate (52–7). Nero decided not to give up the expensive conquest: he too needed military glory, and Quintus Veranius (57–8), who had operated in mountains in Lycia (LACTOR 8, 30), was told to press on into Wales and the Pennines north of the Trent. On his death he was succeeded by Gaius Suetonius Paulinus (58–61), the most distinguished general of the age, first to cross the Atlas Mountains (Dio 60.9.1 = LACTOR 15, p. 92). See Tacitus, *Ann.* 12.31–40.

Only the revolt of 60 prevented Suetonius taking the Druid centre on Anglesey (see Section 3.6 below). Another period of consolidation followed the crushing of that rebellion. From 61 until the beginning of Vespasian's reign little further progress could be made, although Vitellius' appointee M. Vettius Bolanus, a man who had had experience in Armenia under Corbulo (see Section 2.5 below) won some success in the north against the formidable Brigantes (Tacitus, *Agr.* 16.3–5; *Ann.* 14.29–39). Bolanus' achievements were eulogised for the benefit of his son.

39 **Statius,** *Silvae* **5.2.140–9.**
Now if the land your mighty parent reined
in shall receive you, greatly will the wild
Araxes thrill, and glory raise the plains
of Caledonia, when the aged man
who dwells in that grim land shall tell you, 'Here
your father used to give his judgements and
address his troops on heaped-up turf; he gave
lookouts and forts to hamlets – do you see
them over there? – and round these walls dug moats.
And these are gifts he made to gods of war,
these arms displayed; the labels you can still
make out. He put this breastplate on when called
to war; he tore this breastplate from
a British king.'

Vespasian decided that Claudius' prey, kept in part for reasons of prestige, in which he himself had won so much glory, must be brought under complete control, and sent trustworthy, able and energetic commanders to finish the conquest: his kinsman Q. Petillius Cerealis (71–73/4, against the Brigantes and south and central Wales); Sex. Julius Frontinus (73/4–77, north Wales); Cn. Julius Agricola (77–83). His predecessors' ground work enabled Agricola to move beyond the Brigantes. The campaigns ended in 83 at a site in north-east Scotland which Tacitus calls 'Mons Graupius' (*Agr.* 29–38). A veteran's tombstone brings us close to an individual who took part in the occupation; he came from Pannonia, and may have been brought to Britain when the Second, Adiutrix, Legion arrived with Cerialis.

40   MW 384. Lindum.   Titus Valerius Pudens, son of Titus, of the Claudian Tribe, from Savaria, soldier of the Second, Auxiliary, Legion, devoted and loyal, in the century of Dossennus Proculus, aged 30; Afranius his heir placed the stone from his own funds. He is buried here.

By 84 Domitian no longer needed Agricola's successes: he had his own in Germany (see Section 2.1 above). Agricola was recalled to well-earned triumphal decorations, and to retirement until his death (93). His successor is unknown, but the governors that followed were not as distinguished as he and his predecessors: Britain was a back seat compared with Germany and especially the Danube.

Agricola's furthest northern forts, at the southern entrances of the highland glens, were abandoned before 90, most famously that at Inchtuthil, still under construction at the order to withdraw. By Trajan's early years the Clyde–Forth line was held; by the end the line of Hadrian's Wall (122). Settlement in the new positions is shown by the construction of the Wall, and by stone construction further south, as at Caerleon (LACTOR 8, 79). The presence of the Twentieth Legion, previously at Wroxeter, at Carlisle, and only a year later to build a new fortress at Inchtuthil, is attested by a stylus tablet recording a soldier's debt.

41   *AE* 1992, 1139. On wood. 7 November 83.   When Emperor Domitian was consul for the ninth time on the seventh day before the Ides of November. I, Quintus Cassius Secundus, private soldier of the Twentieth Legion in the century of Calvus Priscus, have written that I owe Gaius Geminius Mansuetus, private soldier of the same legion in the century of Vettius Proculus, one hundred *denarii,* which [---]

The main task of the governor and his new assistant, the 'magistrate' (*iuridicus*) who was solely concerned with civil matters, especially jurisdiction and the interpretation of law, was the maintenance of peace within the area of real Roman control and the peaceful extraction of taxes and dues (see Section 3.3 below).

42   MW 311. Urbs Salvia, Picenum.   [To Gaius] Salvius Liberalis [Nonius] Bassus, son of Gaius, of the Velina tribe, consul, proconsul of the province of Macedonia, legate of the Augusti as magistrate of Britain, legate of the Fifth, Macedonian, Legion, member of the Arval Brethren, adlected by the deified Vespasian [and the deified] Titus into tribunician rank and adlected by the same into praetorian rank, quinquennial magistrate four times, patron of the colony.

This man, having drawn the lot for the [proconsulship] of Asia, excused himself from the office.

2.4 North Africa

The title 'the Province of Africa' lacks definition: the whole continent might be meant. This left commanders, originally the third and second century BC opponents of the Carthaginians, later governors of the province, freedom of action. Although it led to few major confrontations, the gradual Roman advance south and west involved a series of small but persistent outbreaks. In 14, at the time Augustus' warning against expansion was read out, roads were being driven further into the province.

43 **EJ² 290. Between Gabès and Gafsa. Milestone of 14.** Emperor Caesar Augustus, son of Augustus, in his sixteenth year of tribunician power. Asprenas, consul, proconsul, member of the seven-man board for the management of feasts, saw to the construction of the road from the winter camp of Tacape.

Similar activity was taking place further east.

44 **EJ² 291. Lepcis Magna. Before 17.** On the orders of Emperor Tiberius Caesar Augustus, Lucius Aelius Lamia, proconsul, laid down the road from the town into the mainland. 44 miles.

Road-building and the marking out of territory (centuriation) uprooted settlements and interfered with the annual driving of flocks and herds north and south in search of pasture. But the rebellion of Tacfarinas (17–24; see Section 3.6 below) only delayed the advance. Under Gaius the command of the garrison, the Third, Augustan, Legion, was separated from the proconsulship and given to a separate legate free to operate in remoter quarters. Its base was moved successively from Ammaedara to Theveste and Lambaesis.

45 **MW 389. Lambaesis. 81** *(restored from a version in which references to Domitian have been erased).* Under Emperor Titus Caesar Augustus, Supreme Pontiff, in his [eleventh year] of tribunician power, eight times consul, [hailed Imperator for the fifteenth time, censor, Father of the Fatherland, and Caesar Domitian, seven times consul, and] under Tettius Julianus, legate of Augustus of praetorian rank, the [Third], Augustan, Legion made the walls and the camp from the ground up.

Towards Hadrian's reign a permanent limit was reached and marked out, the frontier path (*limes*).

2.5 The Parthian Empire and the East

The Parthians took over the remains of the Persian Empire destroyed by Alexander the Great. At first they and the Romans shared an enemy, Antiochus the Great, defeated in 189 BC; then conflict over which power was to control Anatolian dependencies such as Cappadocia and Commagene led to war and to Roman defeats (M. Crassus killed in 53, Mark Antony repulsed with heavy losses in 35). Augustus in 21–19 BC forced the Parthian king to return the standards lost with Crassus and put a Roman nominee on to the throne of Armenia.

The struggle was over prestige, which both powers needed. The Parthian king was vulnerable to rivals, and Roman extortion had already led to the massacre of Italian residents in the East in 88 BC. Augustus' solution was only adequate, and maintaining even that level of control in Armenia meant imposing a new client on the throne whenever one died or was ejected; in 4 Gaius Caesar died of wounds after fighting there; Germanicus Caesar likewise was to die in 19 on a similar mission.

In 17 the East needed more attention: Armenia once again was without a dependent monarch, and the kings of Commagene and Cappadocia had died or been deposed. Tiberius' emissary Germanicus gave Armenia a king, Zeno-Artaxias, who lasted until 35. He incorporated Commagene into Syria, and set up Cappadocia as another province under an equestrian prefect; Roman power had to be demonstrated again in 35 by Tiberius' commander Lucius Vitellius when the Armenian client-king died. (Cf. Tacitus, *Ann.* 2.56–8, 68; 6.40–44; Dio 59.27.3 = LACTOR 15, p. 83.)

46   Dio 58.26.1–4.   At about the same time Artabanus the Parthian gave Armenia to his own son Arsaces, Artaxias having died, and when this brought no retribution from Tiberius against him he made an attempt on Cappadocia and began to behave arrogantly even to the Parthians. |26.2| Some revolted from him as a result and sent an embassy to Tiberius, asking for a king for themselves from among the hostages. He sent them Phraates, son of Phraates, and when he died en route, Tiridates, who was also a member of the royal family. |26.3| To ensure him as easy as possible a takeover of the monarchy, Tiberius wrote to Mithridates of Iberia that he was to invade Armenia, so that Artabanus should leave his own country as he went to help his son. |26.4| That was how it turned out, but all the same Tiridates did not rule for long: Artabanus called in the Scythians and had no difficulty in driving him out. That was the way Parthian affairs went, but Mithridates, apparently the son of Mithridates of Iberia and brother of Pharasmenes his successor as ruler of the Iberians, took over Armenia.

Claudius began well, by sending another pretender to the Parthian throne, but his reign ended with the younger brother of the current Parthian king on the throne of Armenia; to a dynasty producing many sons this throne was useful (Tacitus, *Ann.* 11.8–10; 12.10–21, 44–51). Nero could not afford to leave it ignominiously in the hands of the Parthians. Gnaeus Domitius Corbulo (see Section 2.1 above) was instructed to restore Roman hegemony. He seems to have been governor of Galatia, to which Cappadocia was added, and after two successful campaigns put Tigranes on the Armenian throne; his successor, L. Caesennius Paetus, who was told to annex Armenia, met with a serious reverse. (Cf. Tacitus, *Ann.* 13.6–9, 35–41; 14.23–6; 15.1–7, 24–31.)

47   Dio 62.19.1; 20.1 – 22.4; 23.1–4.   While (Nero) was doing this, a laurelled despatch for another victory came from Armenia. For Corbulo, having gathered the scattered military forces and trained them, neglected as they had been, had thoroughly frightened both Vologaeses the Parthian king and Tiridates, who was ruling in Armenia: they had only to hear news of him ...

[20.1] This Corbulo, then, had taken Artaxata without a struggle and razed the city. After this achievement he made for Tigranocerta, sparing all the territories of those who gave themselves up, but destroying everything belonging to those who opposed him. And he took Tigranocerta, which yielded voluntarily. His other brilliant and glorious achievements ended with his inducing even Vologaeses, formidable as he was, into terms that were fitting for Roman dignity. [20.2] When Vologaeses heard that Nero had assigned Armenia to other rulers and that Adiabene was being ravaged by Tigranes, he began preparations for an expedition in person into Syria against Corbulo, while he sent Monobazus, king of Adiabene, and Monaeses, a Parthian, into Armenia. [20.3] These two shut Tigranes up in Tigranocerta. And when they were doing him no harm at all with their siege, but whenever they came into conflict with him were repulsed both by him and by the Romans he had with him, while Corbulo kept a minute watch over Syria, Vologaeses realistically gave up his expedition. [20.4] He sent to Corbulo and obtained a truce on condition that he sent another embassy to Nero, abandoned the siege, and took his troops out of Armenia. But Nero did not give him even then a speedy or definite reply, but sent Lucius Caesennius Paetus to Cappadocia to prevent any upset in the region of Armenia. [21.1] Vologaeses attacked Tigranocerta and drove off Paetus, who had come to its aid. When Paetus fled he pursued him, cut down the garrison that he had left at the Taurus, and trapped him at Rhandeia, near the River Arsanias. [21.2] And he would have withdrawn without achieving anything, for without heavy-armed troops he was unable to approach the rampart, and he was short of provisions, especially as he had arrived with a huge host without making arrangements for the commissariat. Paetus, though, was afraid of his archery, which impinged on the actual camp, and of his cavalry, and sent him a message to secure a truce. He agreed the terms and took an oath that he would leave the whole of Armenia clear and that Nero would grant it to Tiridates. [21.3] The Parthian was pleased with these terms: he would both get the country without any trouble and have a significant kindness to his credit with the Romans. And learning of the imminent arrival of Corbulo, whom Paetus had been sending for before he was put under siege, he let the Romans go, [21.4] having previously obtained their agreement to bridging the River Arsanias for him; not that he wanted a bridge (he had forded it), but to show them that he was their superior. Certainly even then he did not withdraw by the bridge: he was mounted on an elephant, and the rest forded it as before. [22.1] The surrender was recent when Corbulo arrived at the Euphrates with unbelievable speed and waited for Paetus' forces there. When they encountered each other, you would have been struck by the extreme difference between the armies and the generals: one group confident and preening themselves on their speed, the others depressed and ashamed of the agreement. [22.2] Vologaeses sent Monaeses to Corbulo demanding that he leave the fort in Mesopotamia; the two parties held lengthy discussions on the actual bridge over the Euphrates, after pulling down the central stretch. [22.3] Corbulo promised to evacuate the country if the Parthian would leave Armenia. Each provision was carried out, until Nero was informed of what had happened and negotiated with the envoys that Vologaeses had sent once again. Nero's reply to them was that he would give Armenia to Tiridates, if he would come to Rome. [22.4] He relieved Paetus of his command and assigned the soldiers who had been with him to some other posting.

He put Corbulo in charge of the war against the same enemy ... [23.1] Corbulo was officially making ready to fight Vologaeses, and sent a centurion ordering him to evacuate the country, but privately he advised him to send his brother to Rome. He convinced Vologaeses, who could see that Corbulo's forces were superior. [23.2] Corbulo and Tiridates met at Rhandeia itself; it was a place that satisfied both parties, one because they had cut off the Romans there and let them go under truce, so that it was a visible sign of the kindness the Romans had received, while for Corbulo they were going to wipe out the disgrace that had come to them with the previous agreement made there. [23.3] For they did not just make speeches: a high tribunal was erected and on it images of Nero were set up, and Tiridates, in the presence alike of many Armenians, Parthians and Romans, approached them and did obeisance to them; he offered sacrifice and words of praise, took the diadem off his head and set it by them. [23.4] And Monobazus and Vologaeses came to Corbulo and gave him hostages. And on this basis Nero was saluted Imperator a number of times, and held a triumph, against precedent.

For Tiridates at Rome, see Dio 63.1.1–7.2 (= LACTOR 15, pp. 102–4). The system worked until Trajan's reign, although each side was tempted to score points of the other, Parthia by supporting impostors who pretended to be Nero returning; they began in 69. (Cf. Tacitus, *Hist.* 1.8; Suetonius, *Nero* 57.2.)

48   Dio 63.9.3.   Meanwhile a person pretending to be Nero on the basis of the resemblance he bore to him, stirred up practically the whole of Greece. He gathered a band of ne'er-do-wells and set off for the legions of Syria. But as he was passing through Cythnos Calpurnius arrested him and had him executed.

For feeling about Nero in the East, see Dio of Prusa (with Tacitus, *Hist.* 2.8–9; Suetonius, *Nero* 57.2):

49   Dio of Prusa 21.10.   Even now this matter (Nero's death) is not clear. For as far as everyone else (outside the court) was concerned, there was nothing to prevent him ruling for ever: even now everybody wishes he were still alive. The great majority actually think he is, although in one sense he has died not just once but a number of times, along with those who were quite certain he was alive!

When Vespasian altered the governance of Asia Minor to strengthen Roman control, he removed client kings, including Antiochus IV of Commagene (72/3), and united the kingdom with the province of Syria, while Corbulo's combined province of Cappadocia and Galatia was made permanent. (Cf. LACTOR 8, 70.)

50   Josephus, *Jewish War* 7.220–1, 225–8, 232–4, 236–8, 240, 243.   Caesennius Paetus, then governor of Syria, whether truthfully or acting out of hatred for Antiochus (for really a clear conclusion was never reached), sent letters to Caesar [221] saying that Antiochus with his son Epiphanes had decided to revolt from the Romans, and had an agreement with the king of the Parthians ... [225] Paetus then was believed, and received permission to act as he thought advantageous. He did not hesitate, but suddenly, when Antiochus and his court were expecting nothing, invaded Commagene, leading the Sixth Legion and to reinforce this some cohorts and cavalry squadrons. [226] Aristobulus, king of the region called Chalcidice, and Sohaemus, king of Emesa, as it is named, were alongside him too. [227] The invasion met no opposition: none of the natives wanted to raise a hand against them. [228] Antiochus, when the news reached him without warning, cherished no intention of war with the Romans. He decided to leave the entire realm as it was and withdraw in a chariot with his wife and children. He thought that that way he would clear himself in the eyes of the Romans of the charge that had been brought against him ... [232] For his sons, however, who were young, experienced in war and exceptionally strong, it was not easy to bear the disaster without putting up a fight. Epiphanes and Callinicus, then, resorted to force. [233] The struggle was violent and lasted the whole day. The young men displayed conspicuous bravery and their force was in no way diminished when they disengaged in the evening. [234] But Antiochus, even when this was the outcome of the battle, thought he could not bear to remain. He picked up his wife and daughters and took flight with them to Cilicia, and by doing that he broke the morale of his own troops ... [236] Before they were completely deprived of their allies, then, Epiphanes' suite had to save themselves from the enemy; a total of ten horsemen crossed the Euphrates with them. [237] From there now they rode under safe-conduct to Vologaeses, king of the Parthians, and were not received arrogantly as if they were exiles, but were accorded every honour, as if they still enjoyed their previous good fortune. [238] Paetus sent a centurion to Tarsus, where Antiochus had arrived, and sent him in chains to Rome ... [240] (Vespasian) then gave orders, while Antiochus was still on the road, that he should be released from the chains, abandon Rome as his goal, and stay for the present in Sparta ... [243] Caesar graciously gave (Epiphanes and Callinicus) safe conduct and they arrived in Rome, while their father immediately came to them from Sparta, and they settled there, treated with every sign of respect.

Sohaemus of Emesa also lost his kingdom: LACTOR 8, 59; cf. Dio 59.12.2 = LACTOR 15, p. 71, on Gaius Caligula awarding this and other kingdoms.

There was one disturbance some time in Vespasian's reign that was serious enough to allow M. Ulpius Traianus, the father of the Emperor Trajan, to win triumphal decorations.

51 MW 263. Miletus, Asia. Greek. [--- M. Ulpi]us Traianus, consul, legate of the Deified Vespas[ian and of Emperor Titus C]aesar Vespa[sian Augustus, son of the deified Vespasia]n, [of the province of ---] and of the province of Syria, proconsul of Asia and of Baetican Spain, member of the board of fifteen for the performance of sacrifices, member of the Flavian sodality, awarded the triumphal decorations by decree of the senate.

Whether he had to do much to win them is unclear.

52 Sextus Aurelius Victor, *Liber de Caesaribus* **9.10.** And the king of the Parthians, Vologaeses, was forced by war to keep the peace.

Cf.

53   *[Epitome of Aurelius Victor]* **9.12.**   The king of the Parthians, Vologaeses, was
forced to keep the peace by fear alone.

On the other hand, Vologaeses asked for help from the Romans in checking the
incursions of the Alani, who were akin to the Roxolani ('Red Alans') and active in the
Caucasus and Caspian regions. (Cf. Suetonius, *Domitian* 2.2.)

54   **Dio 65.15.3.**   As to the Parthians, who were at war with a certain people and
asked for a treaty of alliance with him, Vespasian gave them no help, saying that
it was wrong for him to interfere in other people's affairs.

His problems are explained by Josephus.

55   **Josephus,** *Jewish War* **7.244–5, 248–9, 251.**   The tribe of the Alani, Scythians
living round the River Tanais and Lake Maeotis, as I have shown in a previous
passage, [245] took it into their heads at this period to go on a plundering
expedition into Media and country even beyond it. They entered into negotiations
with the king of the Hyrcanians; he commanded the pass which King Alexander
had closed with iron gates ... [248] They made their plundering expeditions with
complete ease, then, and advanced as far as Armenia, laying waste to everything.
[249] Tiridates was ruling it, and he met them and in the battle he fought with
them came close to be taken alive in the conflict ... [251] The brutality of the Alani
was still further increased because of the battle. They ruined the countryside,
drove off a large number of people and other forms of booty from both the
kingdoms, and took themselves back to their own country.

The Romans had long taken an interest in the Iberian kingdom of the Caucasus
(Claudius had replaced one monarch with another in 46: Dio 60.28.7 = LACTOR 15,
pp. 100–1).
    The Flavians restored Mithridates the Iberian king and fortified his stronghold at
Harmozica (LACTOR 8, 60).
    Some time after reviving the combined province of Cappadocia–Galatia
Vespasian sent the Sixteenth, Flavian, Legion, the Firm, to Satala.

56   *AE* **1975, 817 (Suetonius,** *Vespasian* **8.4). From Satala, Cappadocia.**   To the
divine shades. Gaius Quintianus Maximus, standard-bearer of the Sixteenth,
Flavian and Firm, Legion, in the century commanded by Pudens. He lived thirty-
five years. Julia Maxima, his wife and heir, in his memory.

A fort at Apsarus on the Black Sea was created before Vespasian died.

57   **Pliny,** *Natural History* **6.12.**   On the coast before Trapezus is the River Pixites,
and beyond Trapezus is the tribe of the Sanni Heniochi, the River Apsarus with
its fortress of the same name on the gorge, 140 miles from Trapezus.

Under Domitian a centurion was installed near Baku.

58   **MW 369, Beiouk-Dagh. 84–96.**   Under Emperor Domitian Caesar Augustus
Germanicus, Lucius Julius Maximus, centurion of the Twelfth, Fulminata, Legion.

In 106 Trajan annexed the Nabataean kingdom, focus of trade in its capital Petra and link between Arabia proper and Judaea. This made Roman control along the western edge of the desert continuous and firm.

59 **Dio 68.14.5.** About this same time too, Palma, the governor of Syria, took over the part of Arabia that is in the region of Petra and made it Roman subject territory.

The continuity was marked by the construction of a road in 110–11, the Via Nova Traiana from Bostra to the Red Sea (LACTOR 8, 94: milestone from Thoana, 54 miles north of Petra).

In 113 the Parthian monarch Osroes gave Trajan an excuse for war. Pressed by political difficulties at home, he placed a Parthian nominee, Axidares, on the throne of Armenia Major without clearing it with Trajan, as had been agreed in 63–6. Trajan, who may have been looking for a return to Nero's policy of annexing Armenia, marched east. His previous dealings with recalcitrant monarchs had been unequivocally successful; the Alani too, cousins of the troublesome Roxolani, may have been a factor.

60 **Dio 68.17.1–23.1.** After that (the construction of Trajan's Column) he campaigned against the Armenians and Parthians, on the pretext that the king of Armenia had not received his diadem from him, but from the king of Parthia; his real motive was desire for glory. [17.2] When Trajan had set out to campaign against the Parthians and reached Athens an embassy from Osroes met him there, asking for peace and bringing gifts. For when he learnt that Trajan had set out, knowing that he was given to backing his threats up with action, he was frightened, pocketed his pride, and sent begging not to have war made on him. He asked for Armenia to be given to Parthamasiris, another son of Pacorus, and asked for the diadem to be sent to him. [17.3] He said that he had removed Axidares because he was useful neither to the Romans nor to the Parthians. Trajan neither accepted the gifts nor made any other response, apart from saying that friendship is judged by deeds, not words; consequently, when he arrived in Syria he would take all appropriate action. In this frame of mind he journeyed through Asia and Lycia and the neighbouring provinces to Seleucia. [18] When he was in Antioch, Abgarus of Osroene did not put in an appearance himself, but sent gifts and a friendly message: he was afraid of Trajan and the Parthians alike and was keeping on good terms with both, and consequently was unwilling to have any dealings with him ... [19.1] Parthamasiris behaved rather forcefully. Indeed, his first letter to Trajan was signed 'king', but when that elicited no answer, he sent another message, cutting out this title and asking Marcus Junius, governor of Cappadocia, to be sent to him so that he could put in a request through him. [19.2] So Trajan sent him Junius' son, proceeding himself as far as Arsamosata, and, taking it without resistance, arrived at Satala and rewarded Anchialus of the Heniochi and Machelones by giving him presents.

At Elegeia in Armenia he gave an audience to Parthamasiris. [19.3] Trajan was seated on a tribunal in the camp. Parthamasiris saluted him, took the diadem off his head, laid it at Trajan's feet, and stood in silence, expecting to take it back. This was the signal for the troops to salute Trajan Imperator, as if for a victory.

[19.4] ... Parthamasiris was astounded and thought it was done as an insult signalling his death. He turned to flee, but seeing he was hedged round, he asked to speak in private. So he was led into the tent, and obtained none of his requests. [20.1] So he rushed out in a rage and after that out of the camp, but Trajan had him brought back. Going straight back on to the tribunal he told him to say what he wanted in the presence of all. This was to prevent people who did not know what had been said in private from producing contrary reports. [20.2] When Parthamasiris heard this he no longer kept quiet, but said very plainly, amongst other things, that it was not defeated or as a captive that he was present, but of his own free will, thinking that he would not be wronged but receive back the diadem as Tiridates had received it from Nero. [20.3] Trajan made fitting replies to his other points and said that as to Armenia he was not going to hand it over to anyone: it belonged to the Romans and would have a Roman ruler. Parthamasiris, however, could go wherever he chose. [20.4] And he sent Parthamasiris away with his Parthian companions, giving them a cavalry escort to prevent them having dealings with anyone or making any trouble. As to all the Armenians who had come with him, Trajan told them to stay where they were: they were already his to command.

[18.3b] When he had captured the whole of the Armenians' territory and had enrolled the kings who had submitted among his friends, bringing down the unruly ones without fighting, [23.1] the senate voted him many other honours, but also gave him the title 'Optimus', which means 'Best' ...

Trajan's dealings with the claimant are recorded on the coinage.

61   Sm. *N–H* 47. *Aureus,* Rome. 112–14.   *Obverse.* Bust of Trajan, laureate. TO EMPEROR TRAJAN AUGUSTUS GERMANICUS DACICUS, SUPREME PONTIFF, (with) TRIBUNICIAN POWER, SIX TIMES CONSUL, FATHER OF THE FATHERLAND.
    Reverse. Trajan seated on a platform, attended by an officer; Parthamasiris half-kneeling in front of the platform, with Roman soldiers holding standards. THE PARTHIAN KING.

For judgements on Trajan as glory-seeker, and for the murder of Parthamasiris, see evidence from half a century later.

62   Cornelius Fronto, *Principia Historiae* 14–15.   Many hazard the view from his other enthusiasms that for Trajan his own glory would be valued more highly than the lives of his men: he often sent Parthian envoys away empty-handed when they begged him for peace. [15] ... Trajan has not been satisfactorily cleared of the charge of murdering the suppliant king Parthamasiris.

After the takeover of Armenia, Trajan appointed a governor of the united Armenia–Cappadocia.

63   Sm. *N–H* 197. Antium, Latium.   To [Lucius] Catilius Severus Julianus Claudius Reginus, son of Gnaeus, of the [Claudian] tribe, twice consul, proconsul of the province of Africa, legate of Augustus with praetorian rank of the province of Syria and of the province of Cappadocia and Lesser and Greater Armenia, member of the seven-man board that presides over feasts, awarded military decorations by the deified Trajan, the mural, rampart and naval crowns, [four untipped] spears, and four standards, urban praetor, prefect of the treasury of Saturn, [prefect] of the military [treasury], legionary legate of the [Twenty-second], Primigenia, [Legion], devoted and loyal, curator [of the roads --- of -]ia, prefect in charge of the distribution of [grain] by [senatorial decree, legate with praetorian rank of the province of Asia] for two years, [tribune of the plebs (or aedile), quaestor with praetorian rank of the province of] Asia.

Trajan was saved from an earthquake at Antioch, January 115: Dio 68.24.1 – 25.5; his escape confirmed the belief that he was under the protection of Jupiter.

64 Sm. *N–H* 46. *Aureus*, Rome. 112–*c*. 114. *Obverse.* Bust of Trajan, laureate. TO EMPEROR TRAJAN AUGUSTUS GERMANICUS DACICUS, SUPREME PONTIFF, (with) TRIBUNICIAN POWER, SIX TIMES CONSUL, FATHER OF THE FATHERLAND.
Reverse. Jupiter holding a thunderbolt over Trajan. TO THE PRESERVER OF THE FATHER OF THE FATHERLAND.

Trajan continued his campaigns in Mesopotamia (115), which led to the conferment of a second title (LACTOR 8, 99; John Mal. 11.273–4; Arrian *Parthica* 67).

65 Dio 68.23.2 (18.3[b]); 21.1 – 22.2. And when he took Nisibis and Batnae he was named 'Parthicus' … [21.1] Leaving garrisons at key points, Trajan reached Edessa, and there saw Abgarus for the first time. For although Abgarus had sent envoys and gifts to the Emperor on a number of occasions, he himself on different pretexts at different times had never presented himself. Neither had Mannus, the chieftain of the neighbouring part of Arabia, nor Sporacus of Anthemusia … [22.1] When Trajan arrived in Mesopotamia and Mannus sent him a mission, and Manisarus also sent envoys to discuss peace on account of Osroes' campaign against him, saying that he was ready to withdraw from the parts of Armenia and Mesopotamia that he had occupied, Trajan said that he would not trust him until he appeared in person, as he was promising to do, and confirmed his protestations with deeds. [22.2] One of the reasons he held Mannus in suspicion was that he had sent a joint force to Mebarsapes the king of Adiabene and had had it destroyed by the Romans. Consequently Trajan did not wait on this occasion either for them to arrive, but approached them in Adiabene. So Singara and other places were taken through Lusius without a fight.

Provinces were created on the eastern side of the Tigris, and Babylon was captured.

66 Eutropius 8.3.2. He reached the Red Sea (i.e. the Persian Gulf), and there made three provinces: Armenia, Assyria (i.e. Adiabene), and Mesopotamia, along with those peoples who border on Madena (between the Cyrus and the Araxes rivers).

The campaigns.

67   Dio 68.26.1–4²; 28.1 – 30.3. Trajan pressed on into enemy country at the beginning of spring, and since the land near the Tigris does not produce timber suitable for ships, the boats that had been made in the forests round Nisibis he carried to the river on carts; their construction was such that they could be taken to pieces and put together again. [26.2] It was with the greatest difficulty that he bridged the river opposite the Cardyene range: the enemy stood their ground there and were hindering him. But Trajan was well off for ships and troops; some of them were linked together with great speed, while others were moored in front of them with infantry and archers on board, and a third group kept making feints at various places, as if they were going to cross. [26.3] ... The Romans crossed over and occupied the whole of Adiabene, which is a section of Assyria round Ninos; and Arbela and Gaugamela, near which Alexander the Great conquered Darius, belong to this country too ... [26.4²] They then proceeded as far as Babylon itself, and found the country devoid of anyone attempting to hinder them: Parthian power was shattered as a result of civil wars and at that moment was still in dispute among the factions ... [28.1] Trajan planned to divert the Euphrates by canal into the Tigris, so that the boats could go down it and make it possible for him to construct a bridge. But he found out that this river is at a much higher altitude than the Tigris and did not do it; he was afraid that when the stream rushed downhill in a mass the Euphrates might be made unnavigable. [28.2] He used haulage to bring the boats over the very narrow neck of land between the rivers (the whole stream of the Euphrates falls into marshy ground and from there somehow joins the Tigris), crossed the Tigris and reached Ctesiphon. When he captured it he was saluted Imperator and confirmed his claim to the title Parthicus. [28.3] In addition to other honours voted him by the senate he received that of celebrating as many triumphs as he wished. After capturing Ctesiphon Trajan became keen to sail to the Persian Gulf ... [28.4] And the island in the middle of the Euphrates, Mesene, of which Athambelus was king, he brought over with no trouble, but as a result of a storm and the turbulence of the Tigris and the tidal waters of the Ocean, he got into danger. Athambelus, the ruler of the island in the Euphrates, stayed loyal to Trajan, although he was instructed to pay tribute, and the people who lived in what is called Spasinou Charax, which were in the dominion of Athambelus, received Trajan in a friendly way. [29.1] From there he reached the Ocean itself. When he discovered its nature and saw a ship sailing to India, he said that if he had still been young, he would certainly have crossed over to the Indians as well ... [29.3] But after all he was destined neither to get back to Rome again nor to do anything worthy of what he had previously achieved, and beyond that he lost those same things. [29.4] For during the time in which he was sailing down to the Ocean and being brought back again, there were disturbances in all his conquests and they fell away, and either expelled or massacred the garrisons distributed among them. [30.1] ... When Trajan learned of this, he sent Lusius and Maximus against the rebels. [30.2] Maximus was defeated in battle and killed; but Lusius' successes included the recovery of Nisibis, the capture of Edessa by siege and its destruction and burning. Seleucia was also captured by the legates Erucius Clarus and Julius Alexander and burnt. [30.3] Trajan, afraid the Parthians also might make a move, wanted to give them a king, and when he arrived at Ctesiphon he summoned to a large plain all the Romans and all the Parthians who were there at the time, went up on to a high tribunal, and after a boastful speech about his achievements, declared Parthamaspates king over the Parthians and put the diadem on him.

This achievement was celebrated on the coinage.

68   **Sm.** *N–H* **51.** *Sestertius*, **Rome. 116–17.** *Obverse*. Bust of Trajan, laureate. TO EMPEROR CAESAR NERVA TRAJAN OPTIMUS AUGUSTUS, GERMANICUS, DACICUS, PARTHICUS, SUPREME PONTIFF, (with) TRIBUNICIAN POWER, SIX TIMES CONSUL, FATHER OF THE FATHERLAND.
     Reverse. Trajan in military dress, seated on a platform and attended by an officer, placing a diadem on the head of Parthamaspates, who stands in front of the platform with Parthia kneeling beside him. A KING ASSIGNED TO THE PARTHIANS. BY DECREE OF THE SENATE.

It was Trajan's last success. There were risings against the Roman overlords throughout the conquered area, as well as a rising of the Diaspora Jews, surely not coincidental (see Section 3.6 below). Trajan was not well enough, or well enough equipped, to fight again for his conquests. He embarked for Rome, and died on the south coast of Asia Minor on 11 August 117.

69   **Dio 68.30 (75.9.6) – 31.1, 3–4; 33.1, 3.** When Vologaeses the son of Sanatruces was arrayed against Severus' men, before battle was joined he asked for and obtained an armistice, and Trajan sent him envoys and on the basis of the peace granted him a part of Armenia. [31.1] Afterwards Trajan came to Arabia and began to attack the people of Hatra, since they too had rebelled ... [31.3] Trajan sent the cavalry in first against the wall without success, so that they were beaten back into the camp. Trajan himself, riding past, just missed being wounded, even though he had taken off his imperial dress to avoid being recognised. The enemy noticed his impressive grey hair and the gravity of his face and guessed who he was. They shot at him and killed a cavalryman in his escort. [31.4] Crashes of thunder began, rainbows were to be seen, lightning, driving rain and hail, and thunderbolts fell among the Romans whenever they made an assault. And whenever they had a meal, flies settled on their food and drink, causing universal disgust. So Trajan left Hatra, and soon afterwards began to lose his health ... [33.1] Trajan was preparing to make an expedition into Mesopotamia again, but as he began to be worn down by his illness he himself set sail for Italy, leaving Publius Aelius Hadrianus behind in Syria with the army. So that the Romans in their conquest of Armenia, most of Mesopotamia and the Parthians, had lost their labour, and run risks to no purpose. Even the Parthians spurned Parthamaspates and took to being governed in their own way ... [33.3] When he reached Selinus in Cilicia, which was also called Trajanopolis, he suddenly died. He had ruled nineteen years, six months and fifteen days.

His successor, Hadrian, came to power without having been invested with the Tribunician Power and superior military power (*maius imperium*) as a son adopted on Trajan's deathbed with the revolts still in progress.

70   *Historia Augusta, Hadrian* **5.2.**   For when the nations that Trajan had
conquered fell away, the Moors began raiding, the Sarmatians were starting
hostilities, the Britons could not be kept under Roman rule, Egypt was under
pressure from rioting, while Libya and Palestine were showing a rebellious mood.

Even if he had been secure, Hadrian would probably have given up Trajan's
eastern conquests. But it was a turning point. Restraint and consolidation, walls and
careful attention to the state of provincial garrisons became key concerns.

3. How the Provinces were Governed

Up to a point, the parts of the Empire were expected to govern themselves. *Poleis* (city
states) in the East and *civitates* (organised communities) in the West had their own
constitutions which mostly antedated the coming of the Romans.

Rome could not afford large numbers of men to run her Empire, either. Unruly
areas were left to dependent monarchs and put under direct control only after they had
been tamed or if the monarch proved unable to manage or seemed disloyal; such
monarchs, even if they were at the beck and call of the emperor, were powerful figures
to neighbouring cities.

71   **Sm. *G–N* 401. Cyzicus. 37. Greek.**   During the hipparchy of Gaius Caesar, on
the 9th of the month of Thargelion. The people decided, on a unanimous motion
of all the archons. The secretary of the council, Aeolus, son of Aeolus, of the
tribe Oinops, spoke as follows in the central session under the presidency of
Menophon:

Since the new Helios Gaius Caesar Augustus Germanicus has been pleased to
light up with his rays even the kings who are the bodyguard of his leadership, in
order that the greatness of his immortality should increase in impressiveness in
that respect also; while the kings, in spite of much thought on finding a way of
responding graciously to so great a deity, have been unable to discover
appropriate means of recompense for the acts of kindness that they have received;
and the sons of Cotys, Rhoemetalces and Polemo and Cotys, who were brought
up with him and had become his companions and he established them in the
monarchies that were their due from their fathers and forbears: those who are
reaping the unsparing abundance of his immortal grace, who are greater in this
respect than their predecessors because those men had the monarchies by
inheritance from their fathers, while these have become kings and have come to
share the rule with such great deities through the grace of Gaius Caesar, and the
gracious acts of deities differ from inheritances from human beings by the same
degree as day from night and immortal from mortal nature. Having then become
greater than the great and more marvellous than the brilliant, Rhoemetalces and
Polemo have presented themselves in our city to join in the sacrifices and festivals
with their mother, who will hold the games of the goddess, the new Aphrodite,
Drusilla, not only in a fatherland that is friendly, but in one that is really hers,
because she who is both daughter of kings and mother of kings, their mother

Tryphaena, considering this her native land, has fixed the focal point of her home and the good fortune of her life there where she will be fortunate in the kingships of her children, free as they are from the jealousy of the gods.

For its part the people, considering their residence most agreeable, has with all zeal enjoined the archons to bring a decree of welcome for them, by means of which they will thank their mother Tryphaena on their account for the benefits that she has wished to confer on the city, and through which they will make clear also the disposition of the people towards them.

The people has decided to praise the kings Rhoemetalces and Polemo and Cotys and their mother Tryphaena. Upon their entrance the priests and priestesses, having opened up the sacred enclosures and adorning the images of the gods, are to pray for the everlasting life of Gaius Caesar and the safety of these men. All the people of Cyzicus for their part, displaying their good will towards them, having met them with the archons and the garland wearers are to greet them and sit with them and invite them to consider the city their native land and to become responsible for all its good; the magistrate in charge of the youth is also to lead the youths to the greeting, and the regulator of the boys is to lead the free boys there. The decree is to concern both devotion to our Augustus and honour to the kings.

As to provinces, a single senator was normally in charge, one who had held the consulship or the next most senior magistracy, the praetorship, and his duties were both military and civil. The provinces were divided into two categories. Some were assigned to the emperor as part of his provincial duties ('imperial provinces'), and these included all territories acquired under the Principate. These were governed by 'legates', men he selected who were then approved by the senate (*legati Augusti pro praetore*). The ten remaining provinces ('public' provinces) were governed by men with the title of proconsul, no matter whether they had held the consulship yet or not, selected by a combination of seniority and the lot. Egypt, a few entire provinces, and small troublesome districts were entrusted to men of equestrian rank, either because they were too dangerous for senators to be allowed in them (Egypt, with its potential threat to the grain supply), or because they were thought too small to be worth the attention of a senator (e.g. Judaea, annexed in 6, and the Mauretanias). These men bore the military title of 'prefect'. Except in Egypt, whose status was explicitly regulated (Tacitus, *Ann.* 12.60), this title was superseded by the less formal one of 'procurator', meaning a private agent, as the importance of being a servant of the emperor became greater than that of holding a junior rank in the army.

Staffs, apart from any legions, were small. A proconsul had his own legates and a junior magistrate (quaestor) to deal with financial matters, and normally brought a personal group of advisers with him for his year of duty.

An imperial legate's normal term was three years, but might be prorogued (Tacitus, *Ann.* 1.76 and 80). Tiberius' notorious reluctance to replace his governors was seen even in a coveted public province, Asia, which was supposed to be held for one year only: P. Petronius was kept on for six; Pilate enjoyed a decade in Judaea. Various reasons were suggested for this; Tiberius' own explanation, a shortage of worthy men willing to come forward (Tacitus, *Ann.* 6.27), may have been genuine.

3.1 The rôle of the army

The Roman army of about 300,000 men, half legions, the rest 'auxiliary' units (mainly non-Romans who were paid less well and served for 25 instead of 20 years, but received the citizenship on discharge), was able to put up an awe-inspiring display when on the march under a firm commander such as the legions in Judaea had in 67.

72   Josephus, *Jewish War* 3.115–26.   Vespasian, eager himself to invade Galilee, rode out from Ptolemais, disposing his army for the march in the order normal for the Romans. [116] He instructed the light-armed auxiliaries and archers to take the lead, to frustrate unexpected assaults by the enemy and to reconnoitre woods suspected of being potential sites for ambushes. After them came a contingent of Roman heavy-armed troops, infantry and cavalry. [117] They were followed by a detachment of ten men from each century, carrying their own kit and the equipment for measuring out camp-sites, [118] and after them engineers to straighten out irregularities in the road, level difficult places, and cut down woods that were in the way, so that the force should not be worn out by having a difficult march. [119] At the rear of these he positioned his own baggage and that of his staff-officers, with a quantity of cavalry by them to protect them. [120] After these he rode himself, with élite cavalry and infantry and the spearmen. After him came the particular cavalry attached to the legions; for separate groups of one hundred and twenty horsemen are assigned to each legion. [121] These were followed by the mules carrying siege towers and other devices. [122] Then came the legionary commanders and cohort prefects with tribunes, having an escort of élite troops. [123] Then the standards surrounding the eagle, which the Romans have in front of every legion, because it is king of all the birds, and the most courageous. They take it for a sign of empire and an omen that they will be victorious, whoever their opponents are. [124] Behind these sacred objects were following the trumpeters, and behind them the mass of the troops, with a width of six men. One centurion went along with them in the customary way, supervising the order of march. [125] The servants attached to each legion followed the infantry in a single group, bringing the troops' baggage on mules and oxen. [126] Behind all the legions came the mass of the mercenary troops, and behind them followed a rearguard of foot, heavy infantry and a number of cavalry.

Greek theorists and Roman generals wrote about warfare. Flavius Arrian of Nicomedia in Bithynia was both: philosopher and admirer of Xenophon, consul and governor of Cappadocia, he was well placed to notice Roman practices – and adaptability.

73   Arrian, *Tactica* 4.7–9; 5.1; 11.3–6; 33.1–3.   The Romans have cavalry of which some carry pikes and charge in the manner of the Alans and Sarmatians, while others have javelins. [4.8] They have a long, flat sword slung from their shoulders, carry oblong, flat shields shaped like doors, and an iron helmet, a woven breastplate, and small greaves. [4.9] They carry javelins pointed at both ends, both to hurl from a distance whenever this is necessary and to keep in hand when they fight it out at close quarters; and if they have to engage in hand to hand fighting they use their swords. Some also carry small axes with sharp edges all round … |5.1| Each infantry and cavalry formation has its own organisation, commander, number and name, so as to receive the instructions I have mentioned smartly …

|11.3| 'Condensing' is drawing together from a more open to close formation by rank and file, that is by length and depth. |11.4| Shield-locking occurs whenever you thicken the phalanx to such an extent that the formation cannot move obliquely from one side to the other. And from this locking Romans make their 'tortoise', usually square, sometimes round or oblong, or whatever works best. |11.5| Some stand round the edge of the block or circle and throw their oblong shields in front of themselves; others standing next to them throw up their shields so that one overlaps the next and hold them over their heads, |11.6| so neatly putting everything behind a barrier. So they take even spears landing from above, which run off as they would from a roof, and stones big enough to fill a wagon do not shatter the closure but run down it under their own impetus and fall on the ground …

|33.1| And yet I am aware that explaining the name of each unit will be difficult because even the Romans themselves find most of them alien to their native language. Rather, some belong to the Iberian or Celtic language, as they have adapted the actual practices from the Celts: the Celtic cavalry certainly has a superior reputation in battle among them. |33.2| If there are ways in which the Romans are praiseworthy, then they are for this: that they have not been so devoted to their own ancestral customs, but have selected excellent practices from all over the world and made them their own. |33.3| So you would find them having taken even some weaponry from others – they are already referred to as Roman since the Romans made most effective use of them – and martial exercises from others still, and the ceremonial chairs for their rulers, and clothing with a purple border.

But the army played another rôle besides that of maintaining Roman rule in the provinces or cowing peoples beyond them (see Section 1 above). Physically, it constructed forts and the roads and bridges that connected them, although communities had to contribute labour or money.

74 **Sm. *N–H* 414. Milestone *c.* 16 km north of Potaissa, Dacia. 107–8.** Emperor Caesar Nerva Trajan Augustus Germanicus Dacicus, Supreme Pontiff, in the twelfth year of his (tribunician) power, consul five times, hailed Imperator for the sixth time, Father of the Fatherland, made the road, through the First, Flavian Ulpian Spanish, double-strength Cohort of Roman citizens with cavalry attached: from Potaissa to Napoca. 10 miles.

75 **Sm. *N–H* 389. On the triumphal arch on the bridge over the Tagus at Alcántara, Lusitania. 103–4.** To Emperor Caesar Nerva Trajan Augustus Germanicus Dacicus, son of the deified Nerva, Supreme Pontiff, in his eighth year of tribunician power, hailed Imperator five times, five times consul, Father of the Fatherland. (*On the side*) The municipalities of the province of Lusitania, having collected the funds and completed the bridge: Igaeditani, Lancienses of the town centre, Talori, Interannienses, Colarni, Lancienses Transcudani, Aravi, Meidubrigenses, Arabrigenses, Banienses, Paesures.

Socially, the army was important in two ways. First, it was a means of social and professional advancement at all levels, especially if the career involved brought decorations for gallantry. Above this level, the man with a property qualification of *HS* 400,000 could enter the army and hold the three posts that it was normal to hold: commander of an auxiliary cohort of foot, tribune (one of six) in a legion, and finally prefect of a squadron of auxiliary cavalry. The man who had achieved these posts successfully would be qualified to become an official (procurator) in the imperial service (taxation or imperial estates), or a military prefect (*praefectus*) in charge of a military district or even an entire province. The progress of an eques is recorded in the following inscription.

76   **Sm. *N–H* 276. Ferentinum, Latium.**   Titus Pontius Sabinus, son of Titus, of the Palatine tribe, prefect of the first Cohort of Pannonians and Dalmatians with cavalry attached, of Roman citizens, military tribune of the Sixth, Ferrata, Legion, awarded decorations on the Parthian expedition by the deified Trajan: the untipped spear, banner, mural crown; centurion of the Twenty-second, Primigenia, Legion, centurion of the Thirteenth, Gemina, Legion, leading centurion of the Third, Augustan, Legion; placed in charge of the three detachments a thousand strong on the British expedition, from the Seventh, Gemina, Legion, the Eighth, Augustan, the Twenty-second, Primigenia; tribune of the third cohort of the Watch, of the fourteenth cohort of the Urban Troops, of the second cohort of the Praetorian Guard, twice leading centurion; procurator of the province of Narbonensis; member of the quinquennial four-man board with jurisdiction, flamen, patron of his municipality.

Even when a man began as a private soldier he could reach the centurionate.

77   **Sm. *N–H* 300. Matilica, Umbria.**   To Gaius Arrius Clemens, son of Gaius, of the Cornelian tribe; infantryman in the ninth cohort of the Praetorian Guard; cavalryman in the same cohort; awarded military decorations by the Emperor Trajan, the twisted necklet, armbands, chest-pieces, for service in the Dacian War; member of the body-guard of the praetorian prefects; officer of the watch; candidate for the centurionate; curator of the treasury; adjutant to the military tribune; veteran recalled to the colours by the Emperor; centurion of the Third, Augustan, Legion; leading centurion; quinquennial duovir; patron of the municipality; curator of the community. From the city councillors and members of the six-man board of Augustales and the citizens of Matilica.

Second, soldiers mingled with local populations, and *de facto* unions were legitimised when an auxiliary soldier was discharged (**80** below). Not that civilians were always better off for the presence of the military.

78   **Apuleius, *The Golden Ass* 9.39–40.**   The return journey did not turn out well, at least for him (a gardener in charge of the ass), either. A tall person, who was, as his bearing and gear made clear, a legionary soldier, put himself in our path and interrogated us in a supercilious and arrogant tone. 'Where are you taking the ass? It's not carrying anything.' But my master, who was still overcome with grief and anyhow had no Latin, went past him without saying a word. The soldier was quite unable to keep himself from the usual bullying; he took umbrage at my master's silence as though it were intended for an insult, and beat him with the vine staff he was carrying, dislodging him from my back. Then the gardener replied humbly that it was because he did not know the language that he could not make out what he was saying. So therefore the soldier put the question to him in Greek: 'Where', he demanded, 'are you taking that ass?' The gardener replied that he was making for the nearest town. 'But I need to use him. He has got to go with the other animals to carry the baggage of my commanding officer from the nearest fort.' And straightaway he took hold of the bridle that the gardener was using to guide me, and began to pull me away. But the gardener wiped away the blood that had trickled down his head from the wound made by the soldier's blow, and pleaded with his 'comrade' again to treat him with more courtesy and gentleness, lacing his prayers with vows for the success of all his hopes if he did ... [40] But he saw that no amount of pleading was making the soldier any less determined, and that he was inflaming the man's rage against himself; he could see him turning the vine-rod upside down and breaking his head open with the massive knob, and took desperate measures. He pretended to try to grasp the soldier's knees to rouse his pity, got down and crouched over, grabbed both his legs, picked him up and pitched him to the ground with a heavy crash ...

Economically, fortresses provided markets for material goods and services. Townships (*canabae*) grew up round them and might become self-governing communities (*civitates*) and even chartered municipalities (*municipia*). Discharged veterans might continue together after being settled in privileged colonies, as at Cologne and Colchester. Culturally, such clusters of troops with a strong sense of their Roman identity set up a model that locals could copy: the settlers were successful imperialists and, as veterans, privileged citizens.

Units were split up if the situation demanded it, as this interim strength report of an auxiliary cohort of double size (called 'milliary', but with a paper strength of 800) on one side of an oak diptych from Vindolanda behind Hadrian's Wall in Britain shows.

79 *Tabulae Vindolandenses* **II, 90–98, no. 154. About 92–7.** May 18th. Net total of the First Cohort of Tungrians, of which the Prefect Julius Verecundus is commanding officer: 752, including centurions 6. Of these there are absent: seconded on attachment to the governor's bodyguard 46; in the office of Ferox at Coria (? = Corbridge) 337, including centurions 2; at London centurion 1; [---] 6, including centurion 1; [---] 8, including centurion 1; [---] 11; [---] 1; [---] 45. Total absent: 456, including centurions 5. Remaining, present: 296, including centurion 1. Of these sick 15; wounded 6; suffering from eye inflammation 10. Total of these 31. Remainder, fit for service 265, including centurion 1.

The order of magnitude of the figures is sure, but not the exact number of the units. The six centurions surprised the editors of the tablets: ten would have been expected, and they conjecture that the cohort may have been in a transitional stage of enlargement to milliary size. The cohort was contributing to the bodyguard of the governor, which consisted of 500 each of infantry and cavalry stationed in the Cripplegate fort in London. The officer Ferox may be commander of one of the British legions. The writing abraded before the figure 11 possibly contains a reference to a group sent to collect the cohort's pay.

As units settled down in one place they developed ties with the region and were recruited from it, though there were also injections of immigrants from distant provinces.

80 MW 403. Discharge diploma from Moguntiacum. 27 Oct. 90. Emperor Caesar Domitian Augustus, son of the deified Vespasian, Supreme Pontiff, in his ˑtenth year of tribunician power, hailed Imperator for the twenty-first time, censor for an unlimited period, fifteen times consul, Father of the Fatherland, to the cavalrymen who are serving in the four cavalry squadrons, First Flavia Gemina, First of the Canninefates, First of Bodyguards, and of Scubuli, and to the infantry and cavalry who serve in the fourteen infantry cohorts First Flavia of the Damascenes (double strength), First of Bituriges, First of Thracians, First of Aquitanian veterans, First of Asturians, Second of Aquitanians, Second Cyrenaican, Second of Raetians, Third of Dalmatians, Third and Fourth of Aquitanians, Fourth of Vindelicians, Fifth of Dalmatians, Seventh of Raetians, who are in Upper Germany under Lucius Javolenus Priscus, that is who have received honourable discharge after twenty-five years' service or more, those whose names are inscribed below. To them, their children, and their descendants he gave citizenship and lawful marriage with the wives that they had at the time when they were granted citizenship, or, if any of them were bachelors, with those whom they afterwards married, provided each man married one wife only. On the sixth day before the Kalends of November, in the consulships of Albius Pullaienus Pollio and Gnaeus Pompeius Longinus.

To the cavalryman Mucaporis, son of Eptacentis, Thracian. Of the First Cohort of Aquitanians with cavalry attached, under the command of Marcus Arrecinus Gemellus.

Copied down and checked from the bronze tablet which is fixed at Rome in the wall behind the Temple of the deified Augustus next door to that of Minerva.

However, the settlers at Colchester inspired hostile feelings among the displaced and exploited Britons of the area, and became a prime target in the revolt of 60 (Tacitus, *Ann.* 14.32; cf. Section 2.3 above and Section 3.6 below).

What legionaries got for their services to Rome can be seen from a papyrus with fragments of military accounts, showing the nominal roll and daily parade state either of the Third, Cyrenaican, Legion, or the Twenty-second, Deiotariana, 81–96. (Cf. MW 405.)

81 *Military Records* 243, no. 68.
[Column 2]
… Lucius Asinius consul
Quintus Julius Proculus of Damascus

(*in first handwriting*)
[Received] first instalment in the third year of our Lord 247½ drachmas
Out of that were stopped

Fodder	10 drachmas
Victuals	80
Subscription to the camp Saturnalia	20
[?Clothing]	60
Expenditure	182
[Remainder] on deposit	65½
Plus carried forward from the earlier account	136
Making a total of	221½

(in second handwriting)
Received second instalment of the same year 247½ drachmas
Out of that were stopped

Fodder	10
Victuals	80
Boots, socks	12
For the standards	4
Expenditure	106
Remainder on deposit	141½
Plus carried forward from the earlier account	221½
Making an entire total of	343

(in third handwriting)
Received third instalment of the same year 247½ [drachmas]
Out of that were stopped

Fodder	[10]
[Victuals]	80
Boots, socks	[12]
Clothing	145½
Expenditure	247½
Currently on deposit	344

(in fourth handwriting)
Rennius Innocens

[Column 3]
C. Valerius Germanus of Tyre
Received first instalment of the third year of our Lord 247½ drachmas
Out of that were stopped

Fodder	10
Victuals	80
Boots, socks	12
Subscription to the camp Saturnalia	20
Clothing	100
Expenditure	222

(in first handwriting)

Remainder on deposit	25½
Cash in hand	2[1]
Making an entire total of	46½

(*second handwriting*)
Received second instalment of the same year 247½ drachmas
Out of that were stopped

Fodder	10
Victuals	80
Boots, socks	12
For the Standards	4
Expenditure	106
Remainder on deposit	141½
Previous credit	46½
Making an entire total of	[1]88

(*in third handwriting*)
Received third instalment of the same year 247½ drachmas
Out of that were stopped

Fodder	10
Victuals	60
Boots, socks	12
Clothing	145½
On deposit	188
[- - -]	

Pay was a frequent grievance among soldiers; whatever had been decided by the emperor might still not be carried out (for Domitian's pay rise, see **6** above). Nor did discharged soldiers all receive the same rewards.

82   Sm. *G–N* 297(a) and (b). Greek papyrus. Sept. 63.

(a) Copy of the official record. In the tenth year of Emperor Nero Claudius Caesar Augustus Germanicus, 7th day of the month Augustus, in the Great Atrium at the tribunal. There were present in the advisory council Norbanus Ptolemy, officer in charge of jurisdiction and officer in charge of the [Special] Account, Avilius Quadratus and Tennius Vetus [---Atticus, Papirius Pastor, and Baebius Juncinus, military tribunes, Julius Lysimachus, Claudius Heracleides, financial administrator, Claudius Euctemon, Claudius Secundus.

In the case of the discharged soldiers, concerning the citizenship. [Tuscus said]: I have said to you on a previous occasion that the position [of each] of you is not similar nor is it the same: some of you are veterans from legions, some from cavalry squadrons, some from auxiliary infantry cohorts, some from the oarsmen, [so that] the rights of all are not the same; but I shall pay attention to this matter [and] I have written to each of the district generals so that the benefits [of each man] are preserved intact according to each man's rights. [*in another hand*] [---] Written by me.

(b) Copy of a hearing. The legionaries made their approach. On the road of the camp near the temple of Isis. Tuscus the prefect gave us an answer. Do not talk impious sedition [or, impiety]. Nobody is causing you problems. Write on tablets where each of you is billeted and I will write to the generals so that nobody causes you trouble.

On the 4th day of the month Augustus we handed him in the tablets in the camp headquarters, and he said to us, 'Did you hand them in separately, as individuals?' And they said to him, 'We handed them in separately, we the legionaries.'

On the 5th day of the same month we greeted him near the Paliourus and he himself greeted us in return, and on the [7th] day of the same month we greeted him in the Atrium, while he was seated on the tribunal. Tuscus said to us: 'Both in the camp I told you and now I tell you the same thing: the procedure for legionaries is one thing; that of the auxiliary cohorts is different, that of the oarsmen different again. Go on your way, each of you, to your own business, and do not become idle.'

It was of prime importance for the army to be well led, but traditional claims, notably birth, had to be recognised, and so did those of loyalty. The dispute as to whether there was a group of men who might legitimately be called 'military men' (*viri militares*) is best discussed in these terms. There were men who accumulated military experience and expertise, because they enjoyed the life and had seized their opportunities for active service (Agricola was one of these, cf. Tacitus, *Agr.* 5). The emperor, with advice from friends, who had protégés to promote or favours to return, made appointments. Experience was one quality that might make it likely that a man would be selected to serve in the same field again. Agricola was something of specialist in Britain, though he governed Aquitania too, and Funisulanus Vettonianus in the Balkans (**10** above). Extensive knowledge of Greek-speaking provinces, certainly not military experience, qualified Julius Quadratus, from Asia, to control Syria and three legions.

83 **MW 320. Pergamum. Greek.**   Gaius Antius Aulus Julius Quadratus, son of Aulus, twice consul, proconsul of Asia, member of the seven-man priesthood in charge of banquets, member of the Arval Brethren, legate of praetorian rank of Pontus and Bithynia, twice legate of Asia, legate of Augustus of the province of Cappadocia, proconsul of Crete and Cyrene, legate of Augustus of praetorian rank of Lycia and Pamphylia, legate of praetorian rank of Nerva Caesar Trajan Augustus Germanicus of the province of Syria, the August Council of the young men honours its benefactor and permanent president of the gymnasium. Those who took care of the carrying out of the decree were Asclepiades the son of Glycon Myrsicus and Zoilus son of Diomedes and Theon son of Teleson, the secretaries.

Politically, the army was vital to the survival of the emperor.

84 *Historia Augusta, Hadrian* **15.12–13.**   To be sure, when a word Favorinus used was censured one day by Hadrian, and he had given way, his friends criticised him for being wrong in giving way to Hadrian over a word in common use by respectable authors. Favorinus raised a hearty laugh by saying, 'You're giving bad advice, my friends, not allowing me to believe that a man who has thirty legions is more learned than anyone else.'

Vitellius' coins confess his dependence.

85 *RIC* 1², 271, no. 47. *Denarius* **of Lugdunum.** *c.* **March–July 69.** *Obverse.*
Head of Vitellius, wearing laurel wreath. AULUS VITELLIUS GERMANICUS
EMPEROR AUGUSTUS, SUPREME PONTIFF, (with) TRIBUNICIAN
POWER.
 Reverse. Mars advancing, with spear, legionary eagle and military banner.
UNANIMITY OF THE ARMIES.

3.2 Material development

Peace, seriously interrupted only in 68–70, gave opportunities for development,
especially through trade, both within the Empire and outside it. When natural disasters
such as fires or earthquakes caused damage the imperial government was willing to
help.

86 **EJ² 49.** *Obverse.* BY DECREE OF THE SENATE. TIBERIUS CAESAR
AUGUSTUS, SON OF THE DEIFIED AUGUSTUS, SUPREME PONTIFF, IN
HIS TWENTY-FOURTH YEAR OF TRIBUNICIAN POWER.
 Reverse. Tiberius on magistrate's chair. RESTORATION OF THE CITIES
OF ASIA.

The fourteen cities helped by Tiberius (as in 17: Tacitus, *Ann.* 2.47) recorded
their gratitude on a monument.

87 **EJ² 50. Puteoli. 30, later restored.** To Tiberius Caesar Augustus, son of the
deified Augustus, grandson of the deified Julius, Supreme Pontiff, four times
consul, hailed Imperator eight times, in his thirty-second year of tribunician power.
The members of the board of Augustales. Restoration by the community. [Henia?]
Sardes, [?ulloron] Magnesia, Philadelphia, Tmolus, Cyme, Temnos, Cibyra,
Myrina, Ephesus, Apollonidea, Hyrcania, Mostene, Aegae, Hierocaesarea.

Improving communications was a government desideratum for controlling the
Empire, and a wish for all private travellers. The most ambitious scheme, Nero's canal
through the Isthmus of Corinth, failed (Dio 60.17.1–2 = LACTOR 15, p. 107), but
smaller scale achievements were formidable. Road building, primarily for military
purposes, served trade as well, and was of interest to anyone likely to travel (**242**
below). See LACTOR 8, 64, for a milestone of 80 between Ancyra and Dorylaeum in
the province of Cappadocia–Galatia, and there is significant development in the north-
east of the peninsula.

88 **MW 86. Milestone from Melik Şerif in Lesser Armenia. 76.** Under Emperor
Vespasian Caesar Augustus, Supreme Pontiff, in his seventh year of tribunician
power, hailed Imperator for the fourteenth time, consul seven times, Father of
the Fatherland, Emperor Titus Caesar son of Augustus, consul five times; and
[Domitian Caesar, son of Augustus], consul four times. Gnaeus Pompeius
Collega, legate of Augustus with praetorian rank. 3 (miles).

There were also engineering works on the Euphrates.

89   **MW 93. Near Aïni on the Euphrates. 75.** [Emperor Cae]sar Vespasian
Augustus. Supreme [Pontiff], in his fourth year of tribunician power, hailed
Imperator ten times, [consul] four times, designated for the fifth, [Father of the
Fatherland, and Titus] Caesar Vespasian, son of Augustus, hailed Imperator three
times, in his second year of tribunician power, consul twice, designated for the
third time, censors designate, under [Publius] Marius Celsus, legate of Augustus
with praetorian rank; and [Domitian] Caesar, son of Augustus, consul four times
[---] and legion? [...] carried through the work of the mechanical screw, from the
communal [?purse] [...] (*picture of the River Euphrates*) [Third], Gallic, Legion.

Further south a canal in Syria.

90   *AE* **1983, 927. Antioch, Syria. Second quarter of 75** (*though the stonecutter
has made Vespasian imperator twelve times instead of fourteen and awarded
Titus a priesthood he held only as Emperor).*   Emperor Vespasian Caesar
Augustus, Supreme Pontiff, in his sixth year of tribunician power, hailed
Imperator for the twelfth time, Father of the Fatherland, six times consul,
designated consul for the seventh time, censor, Emperor Titus Caesar son of
Augustus, Supreme Pontiff, in his fourth year of tribunician power, four times
consul, designated consul for the fifth time, censor, [Domitian] Caesar son of
Augustus, three times consul, when Marcus Ulpius Traianus as legate of
Augustus with praetorian rank, took care of [the construction] of the course of
the Dipotamia ('Double River') Canal for three miles, with bridges, by soldiers
of four legions: the Third, Gallica, the Fourth, Scythica, the Sixth, Ferrata, the
Sixteenth, Flavian, likewise of twenty cohorts and [likewise?] of the people of
Antioch. One mile.

For the improvement of the public post, hostels were built along important routes.

91   **Sm.** *G–N* **351. About 35 km from Philippopolis, Thrace. 61–2. Greek.**   Nero
Claudius Caesar Augustus Germanicus, son of the deified Claudius, grandson of
Germanicus Caesar, great-grandson of Tiberius Caesar Augustus, great-great-
grandson of the deified Augustus, Supreme Pontiff, in his eighth year of
tribunician power, hailed Imperator for the eighth time, four times consul, Father
of the Fatherland, ordered eating houses and secure accommodation to be
constructed along the military roads by Tiberius Julius Ustus, procurator of the
province of Thrace.

Local authorities and individuals were active in improving facilities and
amenities in their own communities, as at Antioch.

92   **D. Feissel,** *Syria* **62 (1985) 79–84. Greek. Oct. 73 – Sept. 74.**   Under Emperor
Titus Flavius Vespasian Caesar Augustus and Emperor Titus Caesar and
Emperor Domitian Caesar, sons of Augustus. The work of constructing the canal
for fullers, and barriers diverting water from the same river, having been first
conceived by Marcus Ulpius Traianus, legate of Caesar Augustus, was carried
out by the Metropolis of the Antiochians by means of embedded blocks in the
year 122. From the River Orontes up to the [mouth under] Mount Amanus is a

length of fourteen stades, the area of each block is [forty]-one square feet; the assignment of the work was [equal] according to the proportion of the number of men engaged to the length, breadth and depth of each block. Each block which has been worked on will be kept as clean as it was when it was handed over. There are on this pillar the rest of the names of the men in the sector of Damas the high priest: length in feet 33.75; the block of Bagrades 38.25 feet in length (etc.) ... 720 feet in all.

These developments were often ornamental as well as useful: aqueducts, temples, libraries, theatres, amphitheatres, city gates, market-places and administrative and judicial centres (*fora*). Their construction gave employment and enhanced prosperity, and the amenities attracted tourists and worshippers, as assize centres did when the governor presided.

93   **Dio of Prusa 35.15.**   Apart from that, the assizes are held among you (in Apamea–Celaenae in Phrygia, Asia) in alternate years and an enormous crowd of people gathers: people engaged in suits or judging them, orators, officials, flunkeys, slaves, pimps, mule-drivers, shopkeepers, call-girls and workmen. This means that those who have things for sale sell them at the highest price and that there is nothing idle in the city, not the animals under the yoke nor the houses nor the women.

The emperor himself was often credited with provincial buildings although costs were frequently borne by ambitious locals; the people received the amenity and the city the prestige. Domitian actually helped struggling Megalopolis in the Peloponnese.

94   **MW 436. Megalopolis. 93–4. Bilingual.**   Emperor Caesar [Domitian] Augustus [Germanicus], son of the deified Vespasian, Supreme Pontiff, in his thirteenth year of tribunician power, hailed Imperator for the twenty-second time, sixteen times consul, censor for an unlimited period, at his own expense completely restored the arcade for the people of Megalopolis after its destruction by fire.

Vespasian's provincial works were particularly noted.

95   **Victor, *De Caesaribus* 9.8.**   Further, in every country where Roman law runs, cities were restored with pre-eminent elegance, there were massive road constructions, and mountains were cut through on the Flaminian Road to ensure a level path.

In particular, Roman colonies had to be supplied with Roman amenities.

96   **Sm. *N–H* 392. Iader, Dalmatia.**   Emperor Nerva Trajan [---], Supreme Pontiff, holding tribunician power [--- . completed] the aqueduct for the colonists [with his own money], an enterprise on which they had previously spent [--- on the order] of the most sacred leader [---]

A private benefaction might be dedicated to the emperor among other beings.

97 **Sm. *N–H* 395. Athens, in the Agora. Greek.**   To Athena Polias and to Emperor
Caesar Augustus Nerva Trajan Germanicus and to the city of the Athenians, the
priest of the Muses who are lovers of wisdom, T. Flavius Pantaenus, son of
Flavius Menander Diodochus, set up the outer porticoes, the peristyle, the library
with the books, and the entire furnishing, from his own resources, along with his
children Flavius Menander and Flavia Secundilla.

Naturally, cities themselves were concerned for the costs and manpower needed
for their own viability.

98 **MW 336. Statue base from Aquileia. 105.**   To Gaius Minucius Italus, son
of Gaius, of the Velina tribe; member of the board of four with jurisdiction;
prefect of the Fifth Cohort of Gauls (with cavalry attached); prefect of the
First Cohort of Breucians with Roman citizenship (with cavalry attached);
military tribune of the Sixth, Victorious, Legion; prefect of cavalry of the Fifth
Squadron of Elite Troops with Roman citizenship; decorated by the deified
Vespasian with the golden crown and untipped lance; procurator of the province
of the Hellespont; procurator of the province of Asia, which he was entrusted
to govern in place of the deceased proconsul; procurator of the provinces of
Lugdunum and Aquitania and likewise of Lactora; prefect in charge of the
corn supply; prefect of Egypt; priest of the deified Claudius; by decree of the
council.

(*On the side*) Publius Tullius Maximus [and three others], members of the
board of four with jurisdiction, consulted the city senate on 20 May; the decree
was witnessed by [---] Proculus, Gaius Appuleius Celer, Aulus Junius G[---], and
Sextus Cossutius Secundus.

Whereas speeches were delivered in honour of [Gaius Minucius Italus], to the
effect that, a man of the highest distinction, he has turned all the influence or
[power] he has been able to win [as a holder of the highest offices] open to the
equestrian ranks to [enhancing the magnitude and lustre] of his [native city]; and
that he [believes that the tenure of an official post] gives him no greater happiness
[than that opportunity] to work [on its behalf]; with regard to the action to be
taken accordingly, they passed the following resolution:

Since Gaius Minucius [Italus ---] this particular purpose of his merits [---?that]
he has enhanced its natural endowment by the addition of more districts, and
above all it is universally known that it is at his request that the most sacred
Emperor Trajan A[ugustus has decided] that resident aliens who are normally
accounted of our number [should perform] the duties of citizens [along with us];
and that it has come about [through him] that [we enjoy] in particularly full
measure the favour of the greatest of Emperors: it is the pleasure of this council,
and is deemed advantageous to the community, that a bronze statue together with
[a marble base should be erected to him and that] our decree should be inscribed
on the base, so that it [may be] more amply attested that [there is no] other method
open to us of discharging our debts [in a way commensurate with the services]
and benefits conferred by this great man [than by making public] our pride [in
him].

The motion was passed. In the second consulships of Tiberius Julius [Candidus
and Gaius Ant]ius Quadratus.

Vespasian's letter to the Saborenses in answer to their requests has imperial revenue firmly in mind.

99   MW 461. Cañete, between Malaga and Hispalis. 29 July 77.   Emperor Caesar Vespasian Augustus, Supreme Pontiff, in the ninth year of tribunician power, hailed Imperator for the eighteenth time, eight times consul, Father of the Fatherland, sends greetings to the board of four and the councillors of the Saborenses.

Since you indicate that you are in an unsatisfactory condition and labouring under many difficulties, I give you permission to construct a town centre, bearing my name as you wish, on level ground. The income from indirect taxes which you say were assigned to you by the deified Augustus I confirm; if you wish to add any new ones you will have to approach the proconsul about them. I can make no decision when there is no one to present the other side of the case.

I received your decree on 25 July and gave your envoys permission to retire on 29th. You have my good wishes.

The duovirs Gaius Cornelius Severus and Marcus Septimius Severus had the inscription cut in bronze at public expense.

Prosperity was not increasing evenly over the Empire. Some areas apparently suffered from impoverishment and depopulation, notably mainland Greece. Nero, liberating Greece (not for the first time) from Roman rule in 67 (LACTOR 8, 46), regretted that he was not offering the gift 'when Hellas was in its heyday'. Possibly economic difficulties aggravated the problems that the Greeks encountered after liberation.

100   Sm. *G–N* 65. Epidaurus. Greek.   Achaeans and Boeotians and Phocians and Euboeans and Locrians and Dorians honoured Titus Statilius Timocrates, who had been their secretary, for his merit. Since Titus Statilius Timocrates, a man of distinction and of the first rank, whose previous life had been dignified and admirable and who had pursued an excellent political course and when elected secretary after our grant of freedom [in] times that involved crises that were very troublesome and on occasion also dangerous, had undertaken tasks and responsibilities that were too great for a single man and too numerous for one year, by means of which he often put us in an advantageous position [and] set the conditions of our freedom, which were still undirected, on a firm basis. On account of all these things the Assembly of the Panachaeans has decided to praise this person and set up bronze statues of him in the assembly places of the Panachaeans and [in the] sacred enclosure [of Amarios] and in Epidaurus in the shrine of Asclepius, [having] the following inscription: Achaeans and Boeotians and Phocians and Euboeans and Locrians and Dorians honoured Titus Statilius Timocrates who was [their secretary], for his merit.

One of Dio of Prusa's speeches purports to show contemporary conditions in Euboea.

101   Dio of Prusa 7.33–4, 37.   But another man came forward, a kindly person, evidently, from the speech he made and from his bearing. First he asked the crowd for silence. When they were silent he said in a gentle voice that those who were working the uncultivated land and rehabilitating it were not doing wrong. On the contrary it would be right if they found themselves being praised. [34] ... 'For at this moment, my friends,' he said, 'practically two thirds of our country is infertile because of neglect and depopulation. I possess many *plethra* myself, as I imagine some others do, not only in mountainous country but on the plains, and if someone were willing to till them I would not only let him do it for nothing but would gladly pay a fee as well ... [37] So for ten years let them have the land for nothing; after that period let them arrange to pay over a small proportion from the produce, but nothing on the grazing animals. If some non-citizen farms, let this group contribute nothing for five years, and afterwards twice as much as the citizens. And any of the non-citizens who puts more than two hundred *plethra* under cultivation, he is to be a citizen, to maximise the number of keen applicants.'

3.3 'Romanisation' East and West

Few topics attracted as much attention in the last two decades of the twentieth century as 'Romanisation'. The expression was first used in print by the English historian George Stubbs in the mid-nineteenth century. Thereafter, it was used to describe what was considered an admirable process that everyone understood, for the Roman Empire was accepted as a model of the imperialism practised by Britain and other nations.

As doubts set in, the first question was whether 'Romanisation' was a natural, even unconscious process, or something that Romans consciously encouraged. The latter alternative was usually rejected, as little evidence could be found for the Romans as missionaries of higher civilisation. The sons of Gallic chieftains at school in Augustodunum in Gallia Lugdunensis were bettering themselves (Tacitus, *Ann.* 3.43.1); Britons were equally keen.

102 Tacitus, *Agricola* 21. The winter that followed was spent on some very constructive schemes. To let people who were scattered, backward, and therefore given to fighting have a taste of the pleasures of a peaceful and untroubled existence, and so to accustom them to it, Agricola gave encouragement to individuals and assistance to communities in the construction of temples, markets and private houses. If they showed willing he had praise for them, if they hung back, a rebuke. In that way, instead of being put under duress they were spurred on by rivalry for marks of his esteem. [2] Not only that: he was having the sons of the chieftains educated in the liberal arts, and Agricola preferred the keen-witted Britons to the Gauls, cultured though these were; so that the very people who a short time before would have nothing to do with Latin were eager for the training of an orator. Then our way of dressing came to be held in regard, and the toga was often to be seen. Little by little they went astray, taking to the colonnades, bath-houses and elaborate banquets that make moral failings attractive. They were naive: they called it 'civilisation' when it helped to ensure the loss of their freedom.

For an individual success, see Martial.

103 Martial 11.53.

Claudia she, a Rufina, red-headed and
born of the Britons blue-dyed in their woad, but how
well she has taken the heart of the people of the
Latins! What grace in her figure! The matrons whom
Italy bore might well take her for Roman, the
daughters of Athens for one of their own.

In the West, then, 'Romanisation' is used of changes that provincials made in
their existing way of living, for amenity, emulation or ambition: they wanted to be
more comfortable, more like the representatives of the conquering power, or more
acceptable to them; it was very selective and the ruling power itself had already
undergone a similar process of acculturation by absorbing influences from Greece,
especially in art and literature, either through Etruria and Campania or directly.

In the East, Rome's subjects found less to take over. Gladiatorial and wild beast
shows spread in the first and second centuries, primarily in connection with celebration
of the imperial cult (see Section 4 below), to the disgust of some writers, especially
when the shows were at the cultural centre of Greece, Athens, which was vying with
the Roman colony of Corinth.

104 Philostratus, *Life of Apollonius of Tyana* 4.22.   There was another failing that
he corrected at Athens: the Athenians thronged to the theatre under the Acropolis,
intent on the butchering of human beings. Enthusiasm for this was greater there
than it is in Corinth today. Adulterers, rent-boys, burglars, muggers, kidnappers,
and people of that sort were being bought for large sums and brought on. They
used to arm them and tell them to fight each other. Apollonius made an attack on
this too, and when the Athenians summoned him to an assembly he refused to
enter a place that was impure and full of gore. But he said this in a letter, adding
that he was 'surprised that the goddess is not already leaving the Acropolis, with
you pouring out blood of that kind for her benefit'.

Then there was dining.

105 Philo, *On the Contemplative Life* 48–9, 53, 55.   One might perhaps accept the
banqueting arrangements that have now become prevalent everywhere because
people hanker after Italian extravagance and luxury. Greeks and barbarians have
both become very keen on it and make their preparations with the idea of showing
off rather than feasting enjoyably: [49] couches in sets of three, or more, inlaid
with tortoiseshell or ivory and still more costly materials, the majority studded
with gems; coverlets dyed with sea-purple, with gold woven in, others bright-
coloured in every hue to attract the eye; a quantity of goblets arranged according
to their kind: horns, bowls, stemmed cups and others of many shapes, very
skilfully worked with chasing and finished to perfection by men who know their
trade ... [53] Besides these things there are elaborate pieces of confectionery and
roast meats and sauces which chefs and cooks labour over with the idea
of pleasing with their elegance not taste – that was always required – but sight
... [55] Then some dining tables are removed, stripped by the greed of the
guests who gorge themselves like cormorants and even take to eating the

bones; while other tables they foul and scatter and let them go with the food half eaten.

A few changes were imposed: after Bithynia–Pontus had been organised into a province in 63 BC, its cities found themselves with a magistrate, the *timetes* ('assessor'), equivalent of the Roman censor, whose job was to regulate the intake of men into the city council (Pliny, *Ep.* 10.79.3). But most changes were a matter of fashion, as for instance the taste for brick that spread to Asia Minor, to be used in prestigious public buildings. The 'Kızıl aulos' ('Red hall') is still a conspicuous feature on the site of Pergamum, so called for the colour of its brickwork.

3.4 Spread of the citizenship

Associated with these changes, but linked with the ruler's need to reward subjects, was the advance of Roman citizenship at varying rates. Claudius was generous. But he could deprive a man of citizenship if he found his Latin inadequate (Dio 60.17.3–6 = LACTOR 15, p. 95). Vespasian's grant of the Latin right (*ius Latii*) to Spain meant that men who had held the chief magistracies in a community became Roman citizens at the end of their year in office.

106 Pliny, *Natural History* 3.30. To the whole of Spain the Emperor Vespasian Augustus granted the Latin right, which had been tossed about in the storms that the Republic underwent.

Extracts from consequential charters, e.g. on the legal powers enjoyed by the senior male in a family (*patria potestas*), show how closely provincial communities were already conforming to Roman practice, how closely their charters made them follow it, and how anomalies were dealt with. (Cf. the constitution of Salpensa, LACTOR 8, 67.)

107 *Tabula Irnitana* 21 and 97.
 21. *Rubric:* how they may obtain Roman citizenship in that municipality.
 Those who have been or shall be elected magistrates from among the members of the council, decurions and enrolled members of the Flavian Municipality of Irni in the manner that has been provided for in this law, when they lay down their office are to be Roman citizens along with their parents, wives and children born in legitimate wedlock who are in the power of their parents, likewise with grandsons and granddaughters born to a son, each of whom male or female is in the power of their parents; provided that no more are to be Roman citizens than it is appropriate should be magistrates in accordance with this law.
 …
 97. *Rubric:* that patrons are to have the same rights over freedmen and freedwomen who have obtained Roman citizenship through offices held by their children or husbands as they held beforehand.
 As to those freedmen and freedwomen who on the basis of this law have through office held by their children or husbands obtained Roman citizenship, those who have manumitted those freedmen or freedwomen, if they have not themselves obtained Roman citizenship, are to have the same rights over them

and their property as if those freedmen and freedwomen had not obtained Roman citizenship. If the patrons male or female have obtained Roman citizenship, they are to have the same rights over those freedmen and freedwomen and their property as they would have had if those freedmen and freedwomen had been manumitted by Roman citizens.

Grants of consequential Roman citizenship in Spain are recorded.

108   MW 480. Iluro, Baetica.   To Emperor Domitian Caesar Augustus Germanicus: Lucius Munius Novatus of the Quirina tribe and Lucius Munius Aurelianus, son of Lucius, of the Quirina tribe, who obtained the Roman citizenship by holding the office of duovir, (set up the monument) from their own funds, presenting it as a gift.

The benefits of Roman citizenship are famously exemplified by St Paul's experiences at the Roman colony of Philippi.

109   Acts of the Apostles 16.16, 18–24, 35–39.   While we were on our way to prayer a young woman possessed of prophetic power happened to fall in with us. She was providing a good living for her master by divining ... [18] But Paul was disturbed, and turned and said to the spirit, 'I command you in the name of Jesus Christ to come out of her.' And it did so, the same hour. [19] When her masters saw that their prospects of a livelihood had gone they laid hold of Paul and Silas and dragged them to the authorities in the market place. [20] They brought them before the magistrates and said, 'These men, who are Jews, are turning our city upside down, [21] and they are proclaiming a way of life that is out of the question for us to accept or practise, when we are Romans.' [22] And the crowd joined in the attack on them and the magistrates tore off their clothes and ordered them to be flogged. [23] When they had inflicted many strokes on them they threw them into prison, instructing the warder to keep a safe watch on them. [24] On receiving these instructions he thrust them into the inner part of the prison and secured their feet in the stocks ... [35] Next day the magistrates sent lictors with instructions to 'free those men'. [36] The warder reported those words to Paul. 'The magistrates have sent word that you are to be freed: so come out now, and go your way in peace.' [37] But Paul said to them, 'They have flogged us in public without trial, Roman citizens as we are, and thrown us into prison. Are they now going to go on to expel us in secret? No, let them instead come themselves and bring us out.' [38] The lictors reported these words to the magistrates; when they heard that they were Roman citizens they took fright and [39] came in person to mollify them, took them out and asked them to leave the city.

The use of Roman law spread in the provinces, even in the Greek-speaking East. Legates in charge of administering the law (*iuridici*) began to look after the legal activities of government in large and sometimes unquiet provinces.

110   Sm. *N–H* 206. Nedinum, Dalmatia.   To Gaius Octavius Tidius Tossianus Lucius Javolenus Priscus, legionary legate of the Fourth, Flavian, Legion, legionary legate of the Third, Augustan, Legion, juridical legate of the province of Britain, consular legate of the province of Upper Germany, consular legate of the province of Syria, proconsul of the province of Africa, pontiff. Publius Mutilius Crispinus, son of Publius, of the Claudian Tribe, ordered the monument to be set up in his will, to his very dear friend.

The usage of Roman law by soldiers was one medium for its transmission: the following passage is a contract on papyrus between legionaries, found in Egypt, although the transaction took place in Palestine.

111 *CPL* **301, no. 194 (=** *PMich* **7, 445). 188.** In the consulships of ?Publius Seius Fuscianus (for the second time) and M. Silanus, [day and month], in the colony of Caesarea in the winter-quarters of the Tenth, Fretensis, Legion [loyal and faithful: so-and-so, soldier] in the sixth century of front-rank spearmen, has written at the request of [such-and-such, soldier in the same century in the same legion], in his own presence, because he said that he was not literate, that he had received from Petronius, [soldier in the same century] in the same legion [amount of money] which [he will return from his next salary payment ---] either to the lender himself or to his agent [or heir]. If he fails to return this sum to him he shall pay interest at one per cent.

In Egypt the Regulations *(Gnomon)* in 115 clauses that governed the administration of funds acquired from fines, confiscations or unclaimed property, the 'Special Account' *(Idios Logos;* the same title, given to the high official in charge, is translated here as 'Special Accountant'), were affected by Roman law and statutes, notably by Augustus' legislation on marriage and inheritance.

112 *Sel. Pap.* **II 206.1, 8, 18, 28, 34, 54. 150–61.** From the list of regulations which the deified Augustus provided for the office of the Special Accountant, and of the additions to it made under authority, whether by emperors or by the senate or by the successive prefects of Egypt or Special Accountants, I have summarised for you the items in frequent use, so that by committing the concise schedule to memory you may easily master the topics … [8] If to a Roman will is added a clause to the effect that 'Whatever bequests I shall make in the form of Greek codicils are to be valid', it is not acceptable: a Roman is not permitted to write a Greek will … [18] … The deified Vespasian confiscated inheritances left in trust by Greeks to Romans or by Romans to Greeks; however, those who have acknowledged the trust have received one half … [28] If a woman is fifty years old, she does not inherit; if she is less than this and has three children, she inherits, but if she is a freedwoman, four are required … [34] To those in army service and discharged from it it has been conceded that they may make dispositions of property both by Roman and by Greek wills, using what words they choose. But each individual must make his bequest to fellow-nationals and to those permitted … [54] The daughter of a discharged soldier who became a Roman citizen (the prefect of Egypt) Ursus did not permit to inherit from her mother, who was an Egyptian.

Very striking is the archive of documents involving Babatha daughter of Simon, non-citizen, and her family and property: provincials even in this recently acquired province of the Roman Empire apply to the highest authority available to them for definitive settlement of private disputes, in this case over the level of support provided by the guardians of Babatha's orphaned son.

113 *Bar Kokhba Documents* **54–6, no. 14. Greek papyrus with Aramaic and Nabataean signatures. From a cave on the Nahal Hever, south of En-Gedi on the Dead Sea. 11 or 12 Oct. 125.** In the ninth year of Emperor [Trajan Hadrian Caesar] Augustus, in the consulships of Marcus Valerius Asiaticus for the [second time] and Titius Aquilinus, on the fourth day before the Ides of October and [according] to the reckoning of the [province of Arabia in its twentieth year], on the twenty[-fourth] day of the month of Hyperberetaeus which is called [Thesrei] in Maoza in the district of Zoara, Babatha daughter of Simon, son of Manaem [in the presence] of the witnesses [in attendance], through her guardian in this matter, Judah son of Chthousion, summoned John son of Joseph the son of Eglas, one [of the] guardians appointed by the council of Petra for Jesus [her son, who is] the orphan son of Jesus, saying, 'On account of your not having given my son [---] the said orphan [---]. Just as Abdoobdas son of Elouthas, your colleague, has given by receipt, on that account I summon you to take your place [at the] judgement seat of Julius Julianus, governor, in Petra, [metropolis] of Arabia [until we are heard] at the [tribunal] in Petra on the second day of the [month Zeus or at his next presence in Petra. Although [---].' The witnesses in attendance: Johannes son of Makouthas, Sammouas son of Manaem, Thaddaeus son of Thaddaeus, Joseph son of Ananias, [...]as son of Libanus [*traces of three lines in Aramaic?*]. Written by me. (*Signatures on back in Nabataean, Aramaic and Greek*)

3.5 Taxation and misgovernment

Booty and taxation were the immediate and permanent gains of conquest, with taxation taking a number of forms: direct taxes ('tribute') on land and people, collected by local authorities, with Roman citizens being exempted from the poll tax, but not the land tax unless they were natives of Italy or belonged to a specially privileged community; and imperial and local indirect taxes (*vectigal*) and charges, such as customs dues, collected by contractors (the 'publicans'). For local taxes see **99** above. Taxation varied from one province to another.

114 **Hyginus (2),** *On the Establishment of Boundaries,* **in** *Land-Surveyors* **160–1 (203–5 Lachmann).** We ought to survey land subject to tax that is bounded only by natural obstacles and long-standing practice in such a way that it is kept permanently marked out by straight lines and some form of boundary. Many have divided this type of land as if it were the territory of a colony, with lines at right angles to each other – that is, into centuries, as it is in Pannonia. It is my opinion that the measurement of this land is to be carried out by another method. There ought to be a difference between land exempt from tax and land subject to tax. Just as they have divergent status, so the conduct of the survey should be distinct. Our profession is not confined within such narrow bounds that it is unable to direct separate surveys over individual provinces.

Lands subject to tax have many systems. In some provinces they pay a fixed proportion of their produce, some a fifth, some a seventh, others provide money, doing this on the basis of a valuation of the land. Fixed rates of payment have been established for land; in Pannonia, for instance, there is first and second class arable, meadows, mast-bearing woods, common woodland, and pasturage. On all these types of land tax has been fixed by their productivity per *iugerum*. In the valuation of these lands care must be taken over the measurements to prevent habitual usage prevailing after false declarations have been made: in both Phrygia and Asia as a whole there is as much disagreement due to causes of this kind as there is in Pannonia.

Besides regular taxation, booty made a traditional contribution: a one-off construction, the Colosseum, was funded from the spoils of the Jewish War.

115 *ILS* **5633** (*reread by G. Alföldy,* Zeitschrift für Papyrologie und Epigraphik *109 (1995) 195–226, to show how Titus usurped the credit for building it*).   Emperor <Titus> Caesar Vespasian Augustus ordered the construction of the new amphitheatre from his spoils.

Individual soldiers benefited as well.

116   Josephus, *Jewish War* **6.317.**   All the soldiers were so stuffed with plunder that throughout Syria the value of gold for sale was down to one half its former price.

The complex taxation system (on land, persons, crops and other produce, the movement of goods) was normally derived in each region from the pre-existing system. Under the Republic taxes were farmed out to firms of 'tax-farmers' (*societates publicanorum*), who bought the right to collect them for a fixed period of five years, and recouped their expenditure, with a profit, as they collected the tax. The customs law of Asia, published at Ephesus in 62, shows regulations evolving over the years:

117   *SEG* 39, no. 1189, ll. 7, 99–103, 147. Marble slab from the Church of St John, Ephesus. 62 or soon after. Greek.   [7] The law for the dues of Asia on import and export by land and sea ...
[99–103] The same consuls (Gaius Furnius and Gaius Silanus, 17 BC) added: on slaves the publican is <not> to collect for each head more than is [written] in the censorial law: two and a half *denarii* on import, one on export. The same consuls [added: the] publican who has undertaken from the people the contract for the exaction of the dues, in whatever year he accepts the collection of dues, he is to be obliged to discharge them to [the Treasury of Saturn] on 15 October in each year and likewise in the following years on 15 October in each year. The same consuls added: the publican who has undertaken [the] contract for the exaction [of the dues] is publicly to give satisfaction with sureties and pledges of land at the discretion of the consuls Gaius Furnius and Gaius Silanus or of the praetors [in charge of] the Treasury; the appointed day is 15 January next. [The consuls] Publius Sulpicius Quirinius and Lucius Valgius [Rufus] (12 BC) added: the dues on import and export by sea and land by way of the boundaries and harbour of

the colony of Augusta Troas have been excepted [in order that the] colony itself [alone] may exploit them; the rest is to be according to the law ...

[147] (AD 62) If any dispute arises between the person [who has leased this public contract ---] the procurator of Nero Augustus who is in charge of the province [---

Tax collectors practised fraud and extortion and they were hated.

118 St Matthew's Gospel 9.9–12.   And as Jesus was going away, he saw a man, presiding over the customs; he was called Matthew. Jesus said to him, 'Follow me.' Matthew got up and followed him. [10] And what should happen but that as he was reclining in the house, many tax-collectors and guilty men arrived, and reclined alongside Jesus and his pupils. [11] When the Pharisees saw this, they began to ask his pupils, 'Why does your teacher have meals with tax-collectors and guilty men?' [12] However, when Jesus heard them, he said, 'It is not healthy people who need doctors, but those who are in a bad way.'

Violent methods were available to authorities bent on extracting money from debtors.

119 EJ² 117. Greek papyrus from Oxyrhynchus. 11 February 37.   [I, ---] village secretary, son of [---] Eremus [swear by Tiberius] Caesar new Augustus, Emperor, son of [the god Zeus the Liberator] Augustus that I have [no] knowledge of anyone being shaken down in the region of the villages in question by the soldier [---] and his companions. [If I swear truly] may it go well with me, if I forswear myself [the reverse]. Twenty-third year of Tiberius Caesar Augustus, Mecheir 17th.

Misconduct by senatorial governors was catered for by the Julian law of 59 BC, which survived well into the Principate; it was some time before means were devised to deal with equestrian officials (see Tacitus, *Ann.* 4.15, from 23). A speedier procedure introduced by Augustus allowed non-capital offences to be tried by a senatorial committee and completed within a month. The new method, modified, was still in use in the time of Pliny the Younger, available by then to the defendant as well (Pliny, *Ep.* 2.11.3, on his and Tacitus' prosecution of Marius Priscus for extortion in Africa, 100). Even when a prosecution was successful, it did not mean that missing property was recovered.

120 Juvenal 1.46–50.
And here's a governor damned.
The trial was futile. What's disgrace
when cash is safe? – the exile drinks
from tea-time on; yes, Marius loves
it all, the angry gods and all.
But you, the province, won the case
and weep.

For alleged collusion with local politicians, in the first decade of the second century, see Dio of Prusa.

121 Dio of Prusa 43.11–12. But the indictment against me was longer; dare I say grander? A covert affair, evidently! 'Dio stands guilty of failing to honour the gods either with sacrifices or with hymns, thereby abolishing our ancestral festivals; of exerting his influence on a criminal governor so as to get him to torment the people and exile as many as possible, actually to kill some of them by compelling them to commit suicide, because at their age they could not bear to go into exile or give up their native city. He stands guilty even now of collaborating to the full with the man who tyrannised over the province, ensuring (as far as is in his power to do so) that he is successful in his struggle and will get the cities and their popular assemblies forcibly under his control; [12] and of attacking the people itself, getting up as an accuser and using his speeches and his tongue to wrong the citizens, his actual fellow-townsmen; and of doing a number of things which I am ashamed to speak of individually; and of making himself to young and old alike a model of idleness, extravagance and bad faith; and of offering bribes to the people so that nobody will confront him with what was done at that time but will let his hatred and scheming pass into oblivion.'

Whether handling of the provinces improved under the Empire is debated. Performance was variable: extortion was repressed under Domitian according to Suetonius, *Dom.* 8.2, but returned under the following emperors.

122 [*Epitome of Aurelius Victor*] 42.21. Not to mention any other women, it is an extraordinary story how much Pompeia Plotina did to enhance the glory of Trajan. His procurators were causing trouble in the provinces with their false accusations; one of them was said to have approached any rich man with 'Why are you wealthy?'; another with 'What is the source of your wealth?'; and a third with 'Put down your wealth.' Plotina caught hold of her husband and attacked him for caring so little about his good reputation. The effect was that he came to dislike irregular exactions so much that he called the imperial treasury a diseased spleen, because when it grew larger the rest of the body faded away.

Some governors, such as Aulus Avillius Flaccus, began well but deteriorated for external reasons.

123 Philo, *Against Flaccus* 8–9, 17, 21–3. He held the governorship for six years. For the first five, during the lifetime of Tiberius Caesar, he kept the peace and governed so efficiently and firmly as to excel all his predecessors. [9] But in the last year, when Tiberius had died and Gaius had been declared Emperor, he began to let things go and slack off ...

[17] And when the ruler despairs of his ability to keep control, it is inevitable that his subjects rebel against the reins, especially those who are naturally inclined to get stirred up by trivial and ordinary events. Among these the Egyptian race carries off the prize for its habit of blowing up the minutest spark into serious acts of sedition ...

[21] All these people got together and constructed a very cruel plot against the Jews, and approaching Flaccus confidentially said ... [22] ... 'We must find you a very powerful intercessor who will pacify Gaius. [23] The intercessor is the city of Alexandria, which the whole house of Augustus has honoured from the

beginning, especially our present master. And it will intercede if it receives one gift from you; and you will provide it with no greater good than by giving up the Jews and letting them go.'

But there were long-term improvements. Equites and senatorial governors kept an eye on each other (Tacitus, *Agr.* 7.2; *Ann.* 14.38); and the admission of provincial grandees to the senate, where they needed to perform well if they were to advance, may have led to a more caring culture among senators.

The admission of upper-class provincials made it difficult for the aristocracy to keep up a sense of superiority in relation to them, and Pliny the Younger urged colleagues to observe Greece's distinction and sensibilities (Pliny, *Ep.* 8.25). All improvements, however, had to be consistent with the collection of adequate taxes from the province. The comment of Tiberius, made in his early years, and used to justify the good reputation of his 'provincial government', is unforgettable. (Cf. Suetonius, *Tib.* 32.2.)

124   Dio 57.10.5.   And yet he met all these expenditures from regular revenues: he neither killed anyone for their money nor at that time confiscated anyone's property, any more than he used any outrageous methods of levying money. At any rate his response to Aemilius Rectus, governor of Egypt, who once sent him more money than was ordained, was 'I want my sheep shorn, not shaven.'

The public posting system (*vehiculatio*), involved the provision by local communities of facilities for official travellers; and that included the upkeep of roads. The system was abused by Romans and local grandees, although a conscientious governor such as the younger Pliny was careful to avoid issuing travel warrants without justification (Pliny, *Ep.* 10.45–6); there is a plethora of evidence of efforts to check them.

125   S. Mitchell, *Journal of Roman* **Studies 66 (1976) 106–31 and** *Zeitschrift für Papyrologie und Epigraphik* **45 (1982) 99–100. Pisidia. Early years of Tiberius. Bilingual.**   Edict of Sextus Sotidius Strabo Libuscidianus, praetorian legate of Tiberius Caesar Augustus. It is in the highest degree unjustifiable for me in my edict to tighten up regulations drawn up with the utmost care by the Augusti, one supreme among divinities, the other among emperors, to prevent the use of transport facilities without payment. But since there are persons whose lack of discipline calls for punishment here and now, I have put up in individual cities and villages a list of the services that I judge ought to be provided, with the object of seeing it observed, or, if it is disregarded, of backing it up not only with my own power but with the majesty of the best of emperors from whom I received instructions on this very point.

The people of Sagalassus must provide a service of ten carts and the same number of mules for the legitimate purposes of persons passing through, and receive from the users ten *asses* per *schoenus* for each cart and four for each mule; if they prefer to provide donkeys they are to give two in place of each mule and at the same rate. Alternatively, if they prefer to give for each mule and each cart what they were going to receive if they were providing them themselves, they are to pay it to members of another town or village who will actually perform the service, so they may take it on. They shall be obliged to provide transport as far as Cormasa and Conana.

However, the right to use these facilities shall not belong to everybody, but to the procurator of the best of emperors and (?) to his son, a right to use them which extends to ten carts, or three mules in place of each cart, or two donkeys in place of each mule, used on the same occasion, for which they are to pay the fee established by me. Besides them, it shall belong to men on military service, and those who have a warrant, and those who travel from other provinces on military service, on the following terms: to a senator of the Roman people are to be supplied not more than one cart, or three mules in place of the cart, or two donkeys in place of each mule, for which they are to pay what I have laid down; to a Roman eques in the service of the best of emperors must be given three carts, or three mules in place of each, or in place of each mule two donkeys, on the same terms; if he requires more he shall hire them at the rate decided by the person who is hiring them out; to a centurion a cart or three mules or six donkeys on the same terms. To those who are carrying grain or anything else of the kind for their own profit or use I wish nothing to be supplied, nor anything for a man's baggage animals or those of his freedmen or slaves. Board and lodging ought to be provided without charge to all who are members of my own staff and to persons on military service from all provinces and to freedmen and slaves of the best of emperors and their baggage animals, on condition that they do not demand other services free from those unwilling to provide them.

Domitian's later exhortations in a letter to the procurator Claudius Athenodorus show that these efforts were ineffective.

126 MW 466. Hama, Syria. Greek.   According to the instructions of Emperor Domitian Caesar Augustus, son of Augustus, to Claudius Athenodorus, procurator. Amongst the prime subjects, and ones demanding much care from my deified father Vespasian Caesar, I am aware that the privileges of the cities received much concern. With keen attention to these, he gave instructions that the provinces should be oppressed neither by hiring out beasts of burden nor by troubles caused by entertaining strangers. But nevertheless, through complacency or because it did not meet with any correction, this set of rules has not been observed: a long-standing and well-established practice survives to this day, which is gradually passing into law, if force is not used to prevent it prevailing. I instruct you too to pay attention to prevent anyone taking a beast of burden if he does not possess my warrant. For it is the height of injustice either to do a favour to certain people or, because of their standing, that warrants should be written out, when it is permitted to no one to grant them except myself. Nothing then is to be done which will infringe my instruction and will nullify my extremely beneficent attitude towards the cities. For it is just to come to the aid of the provinces when they are not in good condition and hardly adequate to necessary impositions. Nobody is to bring force to bear on them contrary to my wish. Nobody is to take a conveyance except one who has my warrant. If agricultural workers are dragged off, the countryside will remain uncultivated. And you, either using privately owned beasts of burden or hiring them, will do your best [to ---. ---] send signed warrants to you [---]

Trajan improved the system by creating a new official: prefect of transport.

127 Sm. *N–H* 267(a). From Cyrrhus, Syria.   To [Quintus Marcius] Fronto Turbo
Publicius Severus, son of Gaius, of the Tromentina tribe, native of Epidaurus,
leading centurion twice, prefect of transport, tribune of the seventh cohort of the
Watch, tribune of the individual horsemen of Augustus, tribune of the Praetorian
Guard, procurator of the Great Games, prefect of the praetorian fleet at Misenum.
Publius Valerius Valens, son of Publius, of the Quirina tribe, due to his merits
(*sic*).

Trajan made other improvements.

128 Sextus Aurelius Victor, *Liber de Caesaribus* 13.5.   At the same time, with a
view to learning more quickly whatever was being done all over the
commonwealth, intervening staging posts were assigned for use of the imperial
post.

3.6 Revolt in Gaul, Germany, Britain, Africa, Egypt and Judaea

Gaul

Julius Caesar's conquests settled down well, but the cost of eight legions with
equivalent auxiliaries stationed on the Rhine meant high taxation and led to unrest
under Augustus; and although war beyond the Rhine hit Gaul – voluntary donations
were offered by Gaul, Spain and Italy when Germanicus suffered a material disaster
in AD 15 (Tacitus, *Ann.* 1.71.3) – munitions and clothing were less in demand after the
fighting stopped in 16. Over-hasty expansion, partly on borrowed money, brought
nobles into difficulties. In 21 some provoked revolts in their tribes and there was
widespread unrest beyond those four (Tacitus, *Ann.* 3.40–41).

Claudius could ignore it in his speech recorded at Lugdunum (LACTOR 8, 34).
More serious was the outbreak of 68 under the Gallic senator Julius Vindex, for which
several causes have been canvassed. Disgust with Nero is one, but high taxation is the
most plausible (Dio 63.22.1 – 27.1a = LACTOR 15, pp. 108–11). Galba, supported by
Gauls, gave privileges and tax-reductions (Tacitus, *Hist.* 1.8). Consideration from the
government, not freedom from Roman rule, was Vindex's aim. Dependent followers
would have suffered also from harder corvées and less produce sold. Some may have
been disaffected with the entire system, including the benefits normally enjoyed by the
aristocracy; they will have been glad to attack the Romans. There was an element of
'nationalism', with claims of divine backing. Druidism had sunk to a superstition
cherished by have-nots (Tacitus, *Hist.* 2.61).

Galba's rewards left north-eastern tribes, like the Rhine armies loyal to Nero,
disadvantaged and nervous. When the Rhine abandoned Galba in favour of Aulus
Vitellius at the beginning of 69, the Treveri and Lingones joined them (Tacitus, *Hist.*
1.53).

Just as the Gauls in 68 were divided by history and the degree of their dependence
on the legions, so in 70 some found disadvantages in going along with the German
rebels in the 'Empire of the Gauls' (*Imperium Galliarum*): it cut them off from trading
partners in southern Gaul and Britain (Tacitus, *Hist.* 4.69).

The Germans

Vespasian's supporters in 69 enlisted German tribes against the remains of Vitellius' legions left on the Rhine after the invasion force had gone to Italy. Once raised, these tribes, under the Batavian Julius Civilis and Julius Sabinus and the Treveran Classicus, could not be controlled. The Batavians had been forced to serve in the auxiliaries, leaving fields untilled and families destitute. The leaders made themselves out to be liberators, even though they dressed up in Roman uniform and in one case claimed descent from Julius Caesar; it was the Roman Empire dispensing with Rome, as the harangue attributed to the Roman general sent to crush them makes clear (Tacitus, *Hist.* 4.73–4). His massive forces crushed the rebels deserted by Gauls and by waverers such as the Ubii centred on the Romanised Cologne, in autumn of 70.

Civilis was forced into the heartland of the movement, then to the right bank of the Rhine. He entered into negotiations and was allowed to escape; Sabinus and his wife went into hiding and, perhaps because he had assumed the title of 'Caesar', met no compassion: Dio 65.16.1–2.

The Bructeran priestess Veleda, who was a focus of the movement, was allowed to live in Italy, probably as a temple servant.

129 MW 55. Ardea. 78–81. Greek. [Oracle granted to Emperor] Vespasian [Caesar Augustus concerning] Veleda: Do you ask what you should do, [Augustus, concerning this] tall maiden whom the Rhine-drinkers revere, they who bristle [horribly] with the horns of golden [moon?] That you may not keep her in idleness, [let her work] and clean a [little lamp] of bronze.

Britain

While Suetonius Paulinus was attacking Anglesey, eastern tribes, led by the Iceni, rose. Their king hoped to secure his family by dividing his possessions between them and Rome. Nero's officials came to take over, and not only confiscated everything but flogged his widow Boudica and raped his daughters, thus making them unmarriageable and bringing the dynasty to an end. Pent-up hatred against tax-collectors common to Rome's subjects vented itself against everything Roman. The Iceni were joined by their neighbours the Trinobantes. In Trinobantian Camulodunum, another voracious Roman institution reared its massive head: the temple to the Deified Claudius, on whose construction and upkeep the tribes had been spending correspondingly massive sums; in Gaul at least sixty tribes of a better developed region were available to subscribe to the altar that was the model for the one in Britain. Verulamium and the commercial centre Londinium also fell and were devastated; some units of the army were heavily defeated (Tacitus, *Ann.* 14.29–39).

130 Dio 62.1 – 2.2; 7.1; 8.1–3; 12.1–2, 5–6. While this childishness (Nero's) was going on at Rome, a dreadful catastrophe took place in Britain: two cities were sacked and eighty thousand Romans and allied people were destroyed. The island passed to the enemy. And yet all this happened to them at the hands of a woman, so that even on that account they were utterly shamed; this I suppose was the disaster that was divinely foreshadowed ... [2.1] A reason for the revolt was the confiscation of money that Claudius had given to their chieftains: that too had to be returned, or so Catus Decianus said, the procurator of the island. It was on this account, then, that they rebelled, and because Seneca had lent them ten million *denarii* that they didn't want in the hope of a substantial gain in interest, and then exacted it all at once, using force. [2.2] But the woman who particularly aggravated their resentment and persuaded them to make war on the Romans and was considered worthy to lead them and act as commander-in-chief of the whole war, was Boudica, a British woman of royal birth, whose mental capacity was greater than normal for a woman ...

[7.1] After a harangue along these lines, Boudica led her army against the Romans, who happened to be without a commander, their governor having led an expedition against an island called Mona, which lay offshore. This made it possible for her to sack two Roman cities and plunder them and to carry out unspeakable slaughter, as I have said. People who were caught alive suffered every known form of atrocity ...

[8.1] Paulinus, it happened, had already brought over Mona, and when he heard of the disaster on the mainland he left it at once and sailed for Britain. He was unwilling to engage at once with the natives: he was afraid of their numbers and their frenzy. He was minded to put off the battle to a more favourable occasion. But his provisions became short and there was no let-up in the natives' attacks; he was compelled against his better judgement to engage them. [8.2] Boudica, in command of an army of about 230,000, rode in a chariot herself and assigned the other commanders each their own places. Now Paulinus was neither able to stretch his line over against her – so inferior were they in numbers that even if they had been drawn up in a single line they would not have reached – [8.3] nor did he dare to engage the enemy in a unified group in case he were hemmed in and cut to pieces. He divided his army into three so that it could fight on several different sides at once, and made each of the sections strong enough to resist attempts to break through them ...

[12.1] Paulinus addressed them in these and similar terms and then gave the signal for battle, which started the conflict, the natives shouting incessantly and singing threatening songs, the Romans remaining silent and keeping their positions until they were within spear-throw. [12.2] Then, while the enemy were already advancing on them at a walk, they simultaneously made a powerful dash forward on an agreed signal, and in the clash easily broke through their battle order. They were surrounded, though, by the enemy mass, and were fighting on every side ... [12.5] The struggle was a long one, with both sides inspired by the same gallantry and daring. But at length, at a point late in the day, the Romans were victorious, and killed large numbers in the battle, by their waggons and at the edge of the forest, besides taking a large number of prisoners. [12.6] There were plenty, though, who escaped and were making as if to fight again. But meanwhile Boudica became ill and died. Their grief for her was acute, and the funeral spared no expense. The Britons regarded themselves then as truly beaten, and scattered.

The situation remained precarious, and Paulinus' severity led the new procurator Julius Indus, himself a Gaul, to report him to Rome. Paulinus was withdrawn, and his successors, P. Petronius Turpilianus (61–3) and M. Trebellius Maximus (63–9), men with administrative experience, prudently concentrated on reconstruction.

The tribes to the north remained aggressive, and those under Roman control restive. When Hadrian came to power there was a substantial revolt on hand: **70** above.

One possible grievance sounds familiar, if Britons were being recruited into the auxiliary forces (cf. Tacitus, *Agr.* 29.2): this may be the reason for the following military memo, but it may be an intelligence report to a commanding officer and the editors of the tablets prefer to see it as advice from a departing commander to his successor.

131 *Tabulae Vindolandenses* **II, 106–8, no. 164. Wooden tablet from Vindolanda. 97–102/3.** [---] The Britons (?) are without body armour. There are exceedingly many cavalrymen. The cavalry do not use swords, nor do the little Brits mount to throw javelins.

Africa

The recruitment of men into the auxiliaries may have been a grievance in Africa too. Under Augustus there were wars in Africa against the Gaetulian tribes, from which Cossus Cornelius Lentulus won a name for his heirs: Gaetulicus. Under Tiberius in 17 a former auxiliary officer, Tacfarinas, began rebellions that went on for seven years. Tiberius called him a brigand, but had to send in a second legion, the Ninth, Spanish, from Pannonia, as reinforcement. (Tacitus, *Ann.* 2.52; 3.32, 73–4; 4.23–6.)

Taxation was an obvious grievance, especially for people that were unused to it.

132 Dio 67.4.6. Many of the peoples subject to the Romans revolted because money was being extorted from them by force. That was how it was with the Nasamones. They slaughtered the tax-collectors and defeated Flaccus, the governor of Numidia who came against them, so comprehensively that they even plundered his camp. But they found the wine and other provisions in it, gorged themselves and fell asleep. Flaccus discovered this, fell on them, and destroyed them all, even slaughtering the non-combatants. That was enough to make Domitian in his elation say to the senate that he had 'forbidden the Nasamones to exist'.

As time went on some tribes were granted stretches of land of their own.

133 *AE* **1969/70, 696 and** *AE* **1957, 175 (MW 448). Boundary stones from Aïn-Abid, Numidia, and Aïn-el-Bordj (Tigisis).** On the authority of Emperor Vespasian Caesar Augustus, public lands of Cirta have been allocated to the Suburbures Regiani and the Nicibes through Tullius Pomponianus Capito, legate of Augustus.

Further west, in Mauretania, it was left to C. Suetonius Paulinus, the soldier later to defeat Boudica in Britain, to take over the kingdom early in Claudius' reign; the devastation was severe (LACTOR 8, 32).

Continued unrest at the beginning of Vespasian's reign caused him to assign the two procuratorial provinces to a senatorial legate, but they remained vulnerable to unruly elements infiltrating from Spain, even in the mid-second century.

134 MW 277. Banasa, Mauretania Tingitana. 75. When Emperor Caesar Vespasian Augustus was consul for the sixth time and Titus Emperor, son of Augustus, for the fourth, the colonists of the Colony of Julia Valentia Banasa from the new province of Mauretania Africa co-opted as patron for themselves, their offspring and descendants, Sextus Sentius Caecilianus, son of Sextus, of the Quirina tribe, legate of Augustus of praetorian rank for the regulation of both provinces of Mauretania, designated consul.

Sextus Sentius Caecilianus, son of Sextus, of the Quirina tribe, legate of Augustus of praetorian rank for the regulation of both provinces of Mauretania, designated consul, receives into his protection and formal patronage, and into that of his kin, the colonists of the Colony of Julia Valentia Banasa from the new province of Mauretania Africa themselves, their offspring and descendants. The envoys Lucius Caecilius Calvus, son of Quintus, of the Fabian tribe, Lucius Sallustius, son of Lucius, of the Fabian tribe, and [---].

Judaea

The country would have been better left to dependent Jewish rulers to mediate between their subjects and the Romans, but in 6 an inadequate Herodian ruler was removed and a census carried out. Outbreaks began at once, and later rebels claimed family and spiritual descent from Jesus the rebel, though the origins and relationship of Zealots and 'knifemen' (*sicarii*) are controversial. When order was restored, a prefect was installed, his duties to collect taxes and keep the peace. Pilate's priority (26–*c.* 36) was to keep himself in favour with the Emperor, as diverse evidence attests. (Cf. St Mark's Gospel 27.6.)

135 Josephus, *Jewish War* 2.169–70, 175. Pontius Pilate introduced into Jerusalem, by night and muffled up, the images of Caesar which are called standards. [170] At daybreak this caused immense disturbance among the Jews. Those on the spot were flabbergasted at the sight: their laws had been trampled underfoot, as they consider it wrong to set up any image in the city. And at the indignation of the people in the city the populace from the countryside rushed together in large numbers … [175] After that he stirred up another riot by spending the sacred treasure known as the Corban on an aqueduct … At this there was indignation among the people, and as Pilate was in Jerusalem they thronged round his tribunal and shouted him down.

The following inscription is concrete evidence of Pontius Pilate's spending on Tiberius.

136 EJ² 369. To the Emperor, Pontius Pilate, Prefect of Judaea, offered the precinct of the Tiberieium as a gift.

A further period as a dependent monarchy (41–44) came to an end with the death of Agrippa I, and his son, young and perhaps lacking the necessary qualities, was allowed only outlying districts: Gaulanitis, Galilee. The last procurator, Gessius Florus (64–6), is execrated by Josephus, his main offence being a zealous effort to extract overdue taxes. (Cf. Dio 63.22.1a = LACTOR 15, p. 108.)

137 Josephus, *Jewish War* 2.277–9. Albinus' successor, Gessius Florus, made him look highly virtuous by comparison. Albinus committed his misdeeds secretly, for the most part, and under cover, while Florus paraded his transgressions against the nation, and left nothing undone of any kind in the way of plundering and outrage. He was like a public executioner sent to carry out judicial sentence on condemned criminals. [278] When he was dealing with people who deserved pity he was at his most brutal; when he was involved in disgraceful actions he was at his most blatant. There was nobody who smothered the truth with greater discredit, or thought up trickier ways of carrying out his villainous acts. In his view, making a profit out of an individual was petty: he stripped entire cities, wrecked whole populations, and nearly went so far as to make a countrywide proclamation that brigandage was open to all, as long as he himself got a share of the loot. [279] There is no doubt that his greed resulted in all the cities being deserted and in large numbers of people uprooting themselves from their native habitats and taking flight to alien provinces.

In the outbreak of 66 the split between town and country and the inadequacy of the ruling class favoured by Rome were strong factors. The insurgents went straight for the record office in Jerusalem and destroyed the debt records. Religious motives overlay economic strains, justifying violence and all forms of extremism. As the revolt wore on insurgents of one persuasion attacked their fellow-rebels as insufficiently zealous.

138 Josephus, *Jewish War* 5.2, 4–7, 11. 70. While [Titus] was still in Alexandria helping his father to establish the principate that God had recently put into their hands, it happened that the factionalism in Jerusalem came to its height and became three-cornered, as one of the two factions turned against itself. Happening amongst evil men one would call that a good thing, an act of justice …

[4] One would not go far wrong in describing this faction as one born within a faction, and like a rabid wild beast that for want of external food takes to attacking its own flesh. [5] For Eleazar son of Simon, who had indeed been the man originally to segregate the Zealots from the populace in the Temple precinct, withdrew on the pretext of repudiating the outrages daily perpetrated by John (of Gischala) – not that John gave up his serial killings, but actually because he could not put up with being subordinated to a tyrant less well established than himself [6] and was bent on total control and longed for sole leadership. He took with him Judas son of Chelkias, Simon son of Esron, who counted for something, besides the notable Ezekias son of Chobari. [7] A substantial number of Zealots followed each of them. They occupied the inner walls of the Temple, and stacked their weapons over the sacred gate, above the holy façade …

[11] As for Simon son of Gioras, whom the people in its extremity had summoned and brought in with the idea of getting help and made tyrant over itself, he had the Upper City and a considerable part of the Lower, and now began to attack John's followers more determinedly, because they were now under fire from above.

The responsibility for the destruction of the Temple in 70 is shifted from Titus by his admirer Josephus.

139 Josephus, *Jewish War* 6.249–53. Titus withdrew to the Antonia fortress. He had decided to attack in full force at dawn the following day and surround the

Temple. [250] But God had long since condemned it to be burnt, and in the passing of the ages the fated day had arrived, 10 Lous [c. 10 Aug.], on which it had been burnt before by the king of Babylon. [251] However, the Temple's own people were responsible for the flames and they were started by them: when Titus withdrew, the rebels, after a short rest, attacked the Romans again. There was an encounter between the Temple guards and soldiers putting out the fire, who put the Jews to flight and pursued them up to the shrine. [252] That was when one of the soldiers, without waiting for instructions and without shrinking from such an action, was driven by some uncanny impulse to snatch a piece of wood from the fire and, lifted up by one of his fellow-soldiers, to hurl the torch through a golden door which led to other buildings round the shrine on its northern side. [253] The flame went up and a shriek arose from the Jews that did full justice to the disaster. They rushed together to help, giving up all thought of saving their own lives or saving their energy: the object of their previous care was lost.

The final act was the siege and capture of the fortress of Masada in 73, when the garrison committed mass suicide.

140 **Josephus, *Jewish War* 7.389–90, 398, 400–1.**   [Eleazar] wanted to go on with his harangue, but they all cut him short. Filled with an impulse that they could not control they rushed to perform the act. They went off in a frenzy, each one longing to get ahead of the rest; they thought that is was proof of courage and good sense for a man not to be seen among the last. So overwhelming was the passion to butcher their wives, children and themselves. [390] And in fact it was not what might have been expected when they came to the act: they did not lose their keenness ... [398] They died in the belief that they had left no living being from among their number to fall into the clutches of the Romans; but they overlooked an old woman and another related to Eleazar, superior in sense and education to most women, and five children who hid in the underground conduits that carried drinking water while everyone else was thinking only of the killing ... [400] These were nine hundred and sixty, including women and children. [401] The catastrophe took place on 15 Xanthicus [?10 April].

The commander of the siege force, Lucius Flavius Silva, had already fought in Germany, winning high honours, and held the regular consulship of 81 after his return from Judaea in 79 or 80, with a distinguished priesthood to go with it.

141 ***AE* 1969/70, 183ab. From two versions of the text in the amphitheatre of Urbs Salvia, Italy.** [Lucius Flavius] Silva Nonius Bassus, [son of ..., of the tribe] Velina, consul, pontiff, [praetorian legate of Augustus] of the province of Judaea; adlected into patrician rank by [the deified Vespasian and] the deified Titus, censors; adlected by the same into praetorian rank; legate of the Twenty-first, Rapax, Legion; tribune of the plebs, quaestor, military tribune of the Fourth, Scythian, Legion; member of the three-man board in charge of capital sentences; twice holder of the quinquennial magistracy, patron of his colony, in his own name and in the name of [Ann...]tta his mother, likewise in that of [...]milla his wife, at his own expense and on his own land saw to the building of the amphitheatre and dedicated it with forty regular pairs of gladiators.

In the aftermath of the Jewish revolt there were disturbances in Cyrene, 72–3.

142 Josephus, *Jewish War* **7.437–42.** The frenzy of the *sicarii* also took hold of the cities round Cyrene, like a disease. [438] An utter villain called Jonathan, who was a weaver by trade, had slipped through to Cyrene and persuaded a fair number of the poor there to join him. He took them out into the desert with a promise that he would show them signs and apparitions. [439] The only people who noticed these transactions of the charlatan were the prominent Jews of Cyrene, who reported his 'Exodus' and the accompanying set-up to Catullus, governor of the Libyan Pentapolis. [440] He sent soldiers, mounted and on foot, and easily overcame an unarmed crowd. Most of them were killed in the fighting, but some were actually taken prisoner and brought before Catullus. [441] The ringleader in the plot, Jonathan, got away for the moment, but there was a lengthy and extremely careful search all over the country and he was caught. When he was brought before the governor he contrived to escape retribution himself while providing Catullus with a pretext for injustice: [442] his lying story was that it had been the wealthiest of the Jews who had instructed him in his scheme.

Afterwards Agrippa II and his sister and joint ruler Berenice survived in Galilee (LACTOR 8, 61). The government of Judaea was strengthened under a senator of praetorian rank commanding the Tenth, Fretensis, Legion at Jerusalem. Gentile settlements were placed in the countryside and land confiscated; nothing was done to mitigate social problems. A second major rebellion occurred in 117, when Trajan was committed to war east of the Empire, and again involved the Diaspora.

143 Dio 68.32.1–2. Meanwhile the Jews in the area of Cyrene set up a person called Andreas as their leader, and were massacring both the Romans and the Greeks … [32.2] So that altogether 220,000 were killed. In Egypt also similar acts were widespread, and in Cyprus, under the leadership of a person called Artemion, where 240,000 were killed … But Lusius, sent by Trajan, was one of those who crushed the Jews.

144 Eusebius, *History of the Church* **4.2.1–5.** While the business of teaching and the church of our Saviour were flourishing daily and making ever greater progress, the misfortunes of the Jews were coming to a head through the ills they inflicted on each other. Already, with the Emperor (Trajan) approaching the eighteenth year of his reign, a new movement of the Jews sprang up, destroying a very large number of them. [2] For in Alexandria and most of Egypt and also round Cyrene, as if under the influence of some terrible wind of revolt, they were carried away and threw themselves into sedition against the Greeks they lived with. The sedition developed into something big, and the following year they engaged in war on a major scale. (That was when Lupus was governor of the whole of Egypt.) [3] To be sure, in the first engagement they happened to overpower the Greeks, who took refuge in Alexandria, hunted down the Jews in the city and killed them. The Jews round Cyrene lost the support they would have had from them, and systematically laid waste the countryside of Egypt under the leadership of Loukouas and destroyed the local seats of government. Against them the Emperor sent Marcius Turbo with a force of infantry, ships and cavalry as well.

[4] It took some time and a number of battles for him to carry through the war against them. He annihilated many thousands of Jews, not only those from Cyrene but also those from Egypt who had risen with them under King Loukouas. [5] The Emperor suspected the Jews in Mesopotamia too of being about to attack the gentiles there, and assigned Lusius Quietus to cleanse the province of them. He deployed his troops against them and slaughtered a great number. On the basis of this success he was appointed governor of Judaea by the Emperor.

LACTOR 8, 98 is an inscription on a milestone 5 miles from Cyrene which mentions blocking and damage to the road. The coincidence of the outbreak with Trajan's Parthian war is more than that: either Jewish rebels saw their chance or Parthian agents were at work. A vivid sense of present danger is conveyed by the following papyrus.

145   Sm. *N–H* 55. Edict of the Prefect of Egypt. Greek papyrus. 13 Oct. ?115.
[---] They are preparing both fire and steel against us. I know that they are few; but the majority are bringing them in and more powerful people are supporting them, striking bargains so that they should not be abused or plundered. The thing that is hated in a few is justifiably a ground of complaint against the whole city. I know that the greater number of their adherents are slaves. It is on this account that their masters are reviled. For that reason I call upon everyone not to pretend anger when they are after gain. Let them know that we no longer fail to see through them. They are not to have any faith in my good nature, nor to the [..] days [......] we have used violence [..] all that we immediately could, but if anyone wishes to bring an accusation against someone, he has a judge sent for this purpose by Caesar. For it is not permissible even for governors to execute men without a trial, but judgement too has its proper time and proper place, as punishment has its proper form. Let them cease, both those who truthfully and those who falsely say they are the victims of assault, and who are violently and at the same time unjustly demanding justice. For it was possible to avoid being wounded. Perhaps some defence might have been offered for the offences committed before the battle of the Romans with the Jews, but in the present situation judgements are useless, which even previously were impossible. 19th year of ?Trajan, 16 Phaophi.

The effect of the revolt on individuals is graphically shown in the papyri.

146   *CPJ* 2.233, no. 436. Hermoupolis. Aug. or Sept. ?115.   Aline to her brother Apollonius, many greetings. I am in great anguish about you on account of what is rumoured to be happening in the crisis, and because you have left here I have no appetite for drink or food [but] continually stay awake night and day and have one worry: about your safety. Only [my] father's care brings me to myself and, on your life!, I would have lain without eating on the first day of the New Year if my father had [not] come and found [me]. I beg you then, [keep] yourself safe and don't face the danger without a guard. Be like the general here, who puts the burden on to his officers. You [do] the same as well [---] my father [---] for the name [---] of my brother was put forward [---] him. If, then, my brother [---] from affairs [---] write to us [---] to you [---] he is coming up [---] of safety [---]. To my brother Apollonius.

The violence continued in Egypt.

147 Sm. *N–H* 57. Greek papyrus. Hermoupolis. ?116. The one hope we had, and remaining expectation, was the onslaught from our district of hordes of villagers against the unholy Jews. As a result of that the reverse has now happened, for when they encountered each other on the 20th our men were worsted and many of them fell [---] [*3 illegible lines*] However not at any rate [from some] people who have come [from ....] we have received the news that another legion of Rutilius has come to Memphis and is to be expected on the 22nd.

3.7 Local government

Municipal government took different forms, depending on local circumstances and history; a clear picture of it in action in Bithynia is given in Pliny's correspondence with Trajan, *Ep.* 10. In southern Gaul the influence of the Greek colonisation of Massilia is still detectable in the Greek post of agonothete (superintendent of games) that a local magistrate held, and in his post of superintendent (*episcopus*) of the dependent community of Nicaea, while other posts are Roman in title and form (quaestor, duovir, prefect), and found throughout the Roman world.

148 *ILS* 6761. From Nicaea, Narbonensis. To Gaius Memmius Macrinus, quaestor and duovir at Massilia; quinquennial duovir and prefect representing the quinquennial duovir; agonothete; superintendent of the people of Nicaea; from his friends.

The reward for service to the community was commemoration in stone or bronze; Albucianus of Gigthis in Africa obtained Roman citizenship for all who served on the local council, in virtue of the city possessing the greater Latin right (*Latium maius*).

149 *ILS* 6780. From Gigthis on the Lesser Syrtis. To Marcus Servilius Draco Albucianus, of the Quirina tribe; duovir; priest for life; in recognition of the fact that, over and above his many services to the community and his open-handed eagerness to confer benefactions, he has twice undertaken an embassy to the city of Rome at no cost to the community for the purpose of petitioning for the greater Latin right, and has eventually brought news of success, the council decreed the erection of the monument, and although he was satisfied with the honour alone and reimbursed the community for the cost, the people set it up from its own funds.

The official duties of local magistrates are set out in the municipal charters discovered in Spain, notably in the *Tabula Irnitana*.

150 *Tabula Irnitana.* [---] Chapter 19. The aediles ... are to have the right and power of managing the grain supply, sacred buildings, sacred and holy areas, the town centre, streets, city wards, drains, baths, market, testing and adjustment of weights and measures, raising the city watch when circumstances demand it, and if the city councillors or enrolled members of the council deem that anything else besides this is to be done by the aediles, they are to have the right and power of supervising and carrying that out; likewise of taking a pledge from citizens of the municipality and residents, provided it does not exceed ten thousand sesterces per person per day; likewise of prescribing a fine and of imposing a penalty on the same, to a limit of five thousand sesterces per person per day. And these aediles, and those later elected under this law, are to have jurisdiction concerning those suits and between those persons over which the duovirs have jurisdiction, and the right of granting and assigning a judge and assessors, as it is allowed in this law, up to one thousand sesterces. And these aediles are to be allowed public slaves belonging to the muncipality to attend them, clad in the ankle-length skirt ...

Chapter 20. Rubric. On the right and power of quaestors ...

They are to have the right and power of exacting, expending, keeping, administering and regulating the public funds of the citizens of the municipality at the discretion of the duovirs. And they shall be allowed to have with them in the municipality public slaves of the citizens of the municipality to attend on them ...

The charter shows the importance attached to keeping up the fabric of the city:

Chapter 62. Rubric. Nobody is to demolish buildings that he is not going to replace.

No person is to unroof, destroy, or put the demolition in hand of any building in the built-up area of the Flavian Municipality of Irni or of any buildings that are adjacent to that area, that he is not going to restore within the following year, unless it is in accordance with a decision of the councillors or enrolled members, reached when the majority of them are present. Anyone who acts to the contrary is to be liable to pay to the citizens of the Flavian Municipality of Irni a sum of money equivalent to the sum involved, and any citizen of the municipality who wishes and who is entitled to act under this law is to have the right of suing, seeking redress and applying to the authorities for this sum or concerning it.

Precautions were taken against illegal gatherings:

Chapter 74. Rubric. On illegal assemblies, societies and colleges.

Nobody in the municipality is to bring about an illegal assembly, nor is he to form a society or college for that purpose, nor is he to conspire for it to be held, nor is he to do anything that may bring about any of these things. Anyone who acts to the contrary is to be liable to pay to the citizens of the Flavian Municipality of Irni ten thousand sesterces, and any citizen of the municipality who wishes and who is entitled to act under this law is to have the right of suing, seeking redress and applying to the authorities for this sum or concerning it.

Forcing up prices is forbidden:

Chapter 75. Rubric. Nothing is to be bought up and hoarded.

Nobody in the municipality is to buy anything up, hoard it, or agree, join together, or enter into a partnership by which something is sold at a higher price or is not sold or is less readily available for sale. Anyone who acts to the contrary is to be liable to pay to the citizens of the Flavian Municipality of Irni ten thousand sesterces in respect of each instance and any citizen of the municipality who wishes and who is entitled to act under this law is to have the right of suing, seeking redress and applying to the authorities for this sum or concerning it.

Citizens were responsible for contributing to public construction.

> Chapter 83. Rubric. On construction.
> Whatever work or construction the councillors or enrolled members of the council of the municipality have decided is appropriate to be put in hand, provided that not less than three quarters of the councillors or enrolled members of the council were present, and two thirds of those present were in favour, and provided that no more than five days each of work *per annum* should be exacted or decreed from each person and each yoke of animals who are within the boundaries of the municipality, and provided that if any loss is inflicted on anyone in the course of that work or construction, it is paid for from the public funds, and provided that no works are imposed against their will on anyone who is less than fifteen or more than sixty years of age: who are citizens or residents of the municipality who live within the boundaries of the municipality or have a field or fields there, all those persons are to be required to offer, carry out, or provide for those works. The aediles, or those who are in charge of that work or that construction by decree of the councillors or enrolled members of the council, are to have the right and power of imposing those services and exacting them and of obtaining security and of imposing a fine as has been provided and included in other chapters of the law.

The administration of justice must be seen to fit the edict posted by the Roman governor of the province.

> Chapter 85. Rubric. That the magistrates are to have in public the schedule issued by the person who is governing the province and are to administer the law according to it.
> Whatever edicts (etc.) the person who is in charge of the province has published, as far as they relate to the jurisdiction of the magistrate who is in charge of the administration of justice in the Flavian Muncipality of Irni, all those items he is to have published and set up every day for the greater part of the day during his magistracy, so that they may be properly read from ground level; and in the municipality the law should be administered and courts set up, held and administered according to those edicts (etc.); and what does not take place contrary to this law is to take place without malicious intent, as is allowed under this law.

Roman law loomed large even among the citizens of Irni who were not ex-magistrates and so Roman citizens.

> Chapter 93. Rubric. On the rights of the citizens of the municipality.
> Concerning matters on which there is no specific provision or clause in this

law, with respect to the law under which the citizens of the Flavian Municipality of Irni are to deal with each other, in all those matters they shall deal with each other under the civil law under which Roman citizens deal with each other. Whatever does not take place contrary to this law and whatever is transacted which happens or is transacted without malicious intent in respect of this law, that is to be legal and valid.

When there were disputes between cities or on the rights of an individual in a city not his own, the emperor might be invoked.

151 *Aphrodisias* 113, no. 14. Aphrodisias. Greek.   Emperor Caesar Trajan to the people of Smyrna. I wish nobody from the free cities to be forced into your municipal duty, and particularly nobody from Aphrodisias: the city has been exempted even from the provincial schedule, so that it is subject neither to the provincial duties of Asia nor to others. I free Tiberius Julianus Attalus from duty to the temple in Smyrna; he has the highest references from his own city. I have written about these matters also to my friend Julius Balbus, who is the proconsul.

3.8 Provincial failings

There is a story in Dio, which, even if the deaths he mentions were due to disease, suggests a paranoid atmosphere, at least at the time Dio mentions (? *c*. 89).

152 **Dio 67.11.6.**   During this period some people made a practice of smearing needles with poison and pricking with them whoever took their fancy. And many of the victims died without knowing what had happened, but many people were denounced and paid the penalty. And this did not happen only in Rome but in practically the entire inhabited world.

Guarding against disturbances was a constant task of governors, as in Juliopolis (Pliny, *Ep.* 10.77–8). Discontent in the West is shown in 69 by the revolts in Gaul and Germany, and highlighted by the Druidic belief that the burning of the Capitol meant the downfall of Rome (Tacitus, *Hist.* 4.54). Discontent in the East manifested itself in the form of false Neros (**48** and **49** above).

Apart from Roman failings documented above (extortion, brutality), there were failings within provincial societies, sometimes exploited by Rome. Notable was the codification of a distinction between men capable of holding local office and the humbler classes. Hadrian already assumes it.

153 *Digest* 48.19.15.   Venuleius Saturninus in *The Office of Proconsul*, Book 1: The Deified Hadrian forbade that those who belonged to the class of city councillors should suffer capital punishment, except in the case of a person who had killed a parent.

Class and race splits within the cities created financial hurdles restricting membership of the citizen body, as at Tarsus.

154 Dio of Prusa 34.21–3. To move on from Council and People, the Youth and the Elders, there is a considerable mass of people who are as it were excluded from the citizenship. Some people are in the habit of calling them Linen-workers. Sometimes they get exasperated by them and say that they are a mob, a waste of space, and responsible for rioting and disorder, while at other times they consider them part of the city and revise their opinion. If you think that these people are doing you harm and set factional disturbances going, you ought to have expelled them altogether, not allowed them into your assemblies. But if you consider them to be in some sense citizens, not only by residence but because most of them were born here and know no other city, it is in my view unfitting to disfranchise them, and you ought not to sever them from you either. [22] But as it is, since they are abused and taken for foreigners, they are necessarily alienated from what is advantageous to the community ... [23] 'What do *you* tell us to do, then?' Enrol them all as citizens, is what I say, and deserving of equal treatment; do not abuse them, do not cast them off, but consider them part of yourselves, as indeed they are. For it is not true that by being able to put down five hundred drachmas a man can come to love you and immediately become worthy of the city; nor that if a man is poor or failed to procure the title of citizen when someone was enrolling the citizens – a man who was not only born among you, but so was his father and forbears too – he is incapable of cherishing the city or considering it his fatherland; nor that if someone works in linen he is worse than another and that the fact should be thrust in his face and he should be abused for it; while if he is a dyer, leather-worker or carpenter, it is by no means right to make that a subject of abuse.

Even upward mobility, of well-off members of the populace, might be resisted (Pliny, *Ep.* 10.79).

Alexandria was particularly and persistently restive; the capital of a great Hellenistic monarchy, it had lost its position only when taken by Octavian in 30 BC, and the pressure it could put even on governors, if they were weak, is shown by **123** above.

Mainland Greece, with its glorious past, was in particular danger of overestimating its own place in the Roman order.

155 Plutarch, *Precepts for Politicians* 17.7–8, 10 (*Moralia* 814A–C). When we see small children trying on their father's boots and playing at putting on garlands we laugh. But city magistrates foolishly tell the people to imitate the deeds of their forefathers, their ambitious schemes and courses of action that are out of keeping with things as they are at the present time, and put ideas into the heads of the masses. What they do may be laughable, but what happens to them is no laughing matter any more, unless they are treated as negligible. [8] It is not as if there weren't a number of other stories about the Greeks in earlier times for people nowadays to recount and so to help form character and teach sense: at Athens a man might refer not to anything to do with war, but for example to the amnesty decree passed after the fall of the Thirty ... [10] These are things that men can emulate even now and become like their forefathers; but the battles of Marathon, the Eurymedon and Plataea, and all the models that give the masses inflated ideas and fill them with unrealisable ambitions, they should leave to the schools of the sophists.

The danger in which a local politician stood if the populace were roused, as it naturally was by grain shortages, is illustrated by Dio of Prusa.

156 Dio of Prusa 46.8, 11–13, 14. Further, as far as the present shortage goes, nobody is less to blame than I am. Have I harvested more grain that anyone else and shut it up, increasing the price? No. You know yourselves what my estates are capable of producing; that I have sold grain hardly ever, if at all, even when there is a bumper harvest. In all these years I have not even had enough; all my earnings come from wine and cattle-grazing. As to the objection that I lend money but won't provide any for the purchase of grain, I don't have to say anything about that either; you know both types in the city, the men who lend money, and those who borrow ... |11| ... I am saying this for your own good. If you think otherwise you are very much mistaken. [12] If you are going to be like that and if, every time you are in a rage with someone – and in a city you can expect a lot of things to happen, right and wrong – you are going to see fit to avenge yourselves by actually cremating him on the spot along with his children, and force some of his women, persons of free status, into letting you see them with their clothing all torn and going on their knees to you as they would in war; is there any anyone who is such a fool, so misguided, as to choose to live in a city like that for a single day? It is much better to be an exile, to live as an alien in a foreign country, than to put up with behaviour like that. Look, as it is there is the 'reason' that people say you had for turning back from my house – that the depth of the narrow lane made you uneasy – consider what a flimsy thing it is! |13| If it was that that saved me it is already high time to treat the city we are living in as if it were a camp and take over the inaccessible parts of it for future occupation, and the high points or cliff tops ... |14| And nobody is to think that my motive for saying this has been indignation on my own account, nor fear on yours, in case you find yourselves some time accused of being violent and lawless. Nothing in the cities goes unnoticed by the authorities, and by 'authorities' I mean more important ones than those we have here. No. Children who are too unruly at home are reported by their relations to their teachers. It is the same with the populace of the cities when they go wrong: it is reported to those authorities of whom I speak.

Even in the West the lower class might sometime break out, as the case of Mariccus the Gallic rebel shows (Tacitus, *Hist.* 2.61).

Then there was feuding in and between cities (Pliny, *Ep.* 10.82–3), providing governors with an opportunity to play off one side against the other, as Dio of Prusa warned.

157 Dio of Prusa 38.36. As to how it stands with your governors, what need is there to talk of it? You know. Or is it possible that you are not aware of the arbitrary power that your quarrelling puts in the hands of your governors? Straight off the man who wants to ill-treat the province comes knowing what he has to do to avoid paying the penalty. He either attaches himself to the Nicaean faction and has their group to help him, or he chooses the Nicomedians and is saved by you. And while he has no care for either side, he seems to have some for one or the other, even as he mistreats them all. Yet even as he mistreats them he is saved by the people who have the idea that they alone are the ones he cares for.

The civil wars of 68–9 gave feuding cities a chance to pay off old scores (Tacitus, *Hist.* 1.69 and 4.50). Dio of Prusa tried to make the people of Tarsus better disposed towards the other cities of Cilicia Pedias.

158 Dio of Prusa 34.47–8. So with the other cities too. I think that you should treat them with kindness and care, with the idea of winning their respect, not as if you hated them. If you do, everyone will be your willing followers and will offer you admiration and affection; and that means more than that Mallus should offer sacrifice and conduct its law suits in your city. There is no advantage to you whatsoever in the people of Adana or Aegeae coming here to offer sacrifice; just vanity, self-deception, and silly, useless ambition. [48] But good will and being seen to be exceptionally worthy and generous, those are the things that are really good, those are worth competing for and taking seriously. And you had better pay attention to them: your present concerns are a laughing stock. And whether it is the people of Aegeae feuding against you or the Apameans with the people of Antioch or further afield the Smyrniotes against the Ephesians, the quarrel is over a donkey's shadow; primacy and power are in other hands.

Boundary disputes were especially common:

159 MW 446. On Col de la Forclaz, between Chamonix and St Gervais les Bains.
74. On the authority of Emperor Caesar Vespasian Augustus, Supreme Pontiff, in his fifth year of tribunician power, five time consul, designated consul for the sixth time, Father of the Fatherland, Gnaeus Pinarius Cornelius Clemens, his legate of the Upper German army, set the boundary stones between the people of Vienna and the Ceutrones.

The concord between cities mentioned on coins and inscriptions could signify commercial alliances and the use of a common mint as well as good will.

160 MW 498. Bronze coin of Ephesus, Asia. Greek. *Obverse.* Head of Domitian, laureate, with aegis. DOMITIAN CAESAR AUGUSTUS GERMANICUS.
    Reverse. Statue of Ephesian Artemis between two figures of Nemesis. UNDER THE PROCONSULSHIP OF RUSO. CONCORD OF EPHESIANS AND SMYRNIOTES.

Extravagance in spending was another failing, both on city projects (Pliny, *Ep.* 10.37–8), and on embassies to impress the overlords (Pliny, *Ep.* 10.43). Financial integrity was exceptional, and public funds devoted to endowments were liable to be embezzled: at Acmonia the deceased benefactor Titus Flavius Praxias was honoured in a Roman ceremony, the Rosalia, and his establishment was guaranteed by the permanence of the Empire itself, and by the cult of the deified emperors; infringement would seem disloyal; at the same time Acmonia displayed its connexion with the greatest Greek city in the neighbourhood, Ephesus.

161 MW 500. Acmonia, Asia. 85. Greek. [---] and that six freedmen appointed by Praxias to his monument are to share in the distribution and to [?participate on an equal basis]; and that there are to be counted, in the [place] of those deceased, persons who are of their descent to the number of six. The feast is to take place on the festal day of the month Panemus, and from the revenue from this endowment roses to the value of twelve *denarii* are to be borne to the monument of Praxias by the city magistrates and the secretary of the council. The council and all the persons appointed to the annual magistracies are to provide for the freedmen and to make sure that no part of this monument or the plants or buildings round it are damaged or alienated in any way whatsoever.

This decree of the people has become law and is to be maintained for as long as the hegemony of the Romans shall last, and nobody shall have the power to change any part of what has been decreed or amend it or divert it to any other purpose in any way whatsoever. All persons jointly and severally are to provide for the maintenance of the decrees passed by common consent and inviolate in accordance with the disposition made by Titus Praxias: 'And for me alone it is permissible to change anything inscribed in the decree or to correct anything or to make arrangements additional to those inscribed.'

It is particularly provided in all the council resolutions that only councillors who are present and taking part in the feast may have a share in this distribution, calling collectively and individually on the deified Augusti and our ancestral deities, Zeus Stodmenus, Asclepius the Saviour and Artemis of Ephesus, to witness and oversee and act as protectors of what has [thus] been decreed. The secretary of the council and priest Asclepiades is called upon also after his current year of office to take care in perpetuity of the [?gifts] and dispositions made by Praxias, just as he was called upon [by Praxias] to do.

The duty of drafting the decree fell upon Ponticus the son of Diophantus, Hecataeus the son of Ponticus, and Alexander [---]. It was passed (or, validated) on 5 March in the eleventh [consulship] of Domitian Caesar Augustus Germanicus, in the [year 16]9 of our era, on the thirteenth day of the month Xandicus, [and was inscribed] by the hand of Hermogenes, public slave.

Poor record keeping gave trouble in Egypt.

162 *POxy* II 237, col. 8, 27–43. Oxyrhynchus. Greek papyrus. 89. Proclamation of Marcus Mettius Rufus, Prefect of Egypt. Claudius Areius, officer of the Oxyrhynchite district, has demonstrated to me that neither private nor public affairs are suitably organised because for many years the official abstracts in the property record office have not been kept in the proper way, even though there were frequent decisions on the part of my predecessors that they should receive the necessary correction. It is not feasible to do this properly without copies going back to the past. I therefore order all property owners to register their own possession with the property record office within six months; creditors any mortgages they have, and others any claims they may have. When they make their return they are to declare the source of each item of property or possession that has come to them.

Wives too are to be appended to the declaration of their husbands if in accordance with local law his property is liable to a claim by them, and children likewise in the property declarations of their parents where usufruct has been guaranteed to the parents through public contracts but ownership after their death has been secured to the children, so that those who enter into contracts with them are not misled by ignorance.

I also enjoin the clerks who draw up contracts and the recorders to [finalise] nothing without instructions from the property record office. They are informed that anything of that kind will not be valid and further that they themselves if they act contrary to instructions will have to expect the appropriate penalty. If in the property record office there are registrations from earlier times, they are to be most carefully protected and likewise the abstracts, in order that if there is any further investigation into those who have made irregular registrations, they may be convicted by these means.

[Therefore in order that] the use of the abstracts may be secure and preserved in perpetuity, making a second registration unnecessary, I enjoin the keepers of the record office to review the abstracts every five years, transferring to freshly made ones those of the most recent property statement of each individual by village and by category. In the ninth year of Domitian, 4th day of the month Domitian.

Senators and equites were commissioned as *curatores civitatis* (community curators) to prevent local mismanagement of funds.

163 *Digest* **50.9.4, Intro. and 1.** Ulpian in his monograph *The Functions of the Corporation Curator.*

Self-seeking decrees of the city councillors ought to be rescinded; on the same basis, then, equally if, as they are inclined to do, they have discharged someone who is a debtor or if they have distributed largesse (9.4.1) or if they have decreed that something is to be given from the public fund to an individual, whether landed property or a building or a fixed sum of money, no decree of this kind shall be valid.

As to material welfare, there is plentiful evidence for grain shortages, as in Asia Minor in the early nineties.

164 **MW 464. Pisidian Antioch, Galatia.** [Col. 1] To Lucius Antistius Rusticus, son of [Lucius], of the Galerian tribe; consul; propraetorian legate to Emperor Caesar [Domitian] Augustus [Germanicus] of the provinces of Cappadocia, Galatia, Pontus, Pisidia, Paphlagonia, Armenia Minor and Lycaonia; prefect of the Treasury of Saturn; proconsul of the province of Further Spain; legate of the deified Vespasian and of the deified Titus and of Emperor Caesar [Domitian] Augustus [Germanicus] of the Eighth, Augustan, Legion; curator of the Aurelian and Cornelian roads; co-opted among the senators of praetorian rank by the deified Vespasian and the deified Titus; awarded military decorations by them, the mural crown, the fortification crown, the golden crown, three banners and three untipped lances; military tribune of the Second, Augustan, Legion; member of the judicial board of fifteen; patron of the colony: for his diligence in providing for the grain supply.

[Col. 2] Edict of Lucius Antistius Rusticus, praetorian legate of Emperor Caesar Domitian Augustus Germanicus: Since the duovirs and members of the council of the most splendid colony of Antioch have written to me saying that the harshness of the winter has caused the price of grain to rocket, and have requested that the mass of ordinary people should have some means of buying it

(*In margin:* ?Good luck!), all persons who are either citizens or resident aliens of the colony of Antioch are to declare before the duovirs of the colony of Antioch within thirty days of the posting of my edict how much grain each has and where it is, and how much he is drawing for seed or for the annual supply of his household; and he is to make all the rest of the grain available to the buyers of the colony of Antioch. I appoint a period for selling to end on 1 August next. If anyone fails to act accordingly, let him know that for whatever is kept contrary to my edict, I shall impose penalties for the offence, establishing an eighth share as the amount to be allocated as the reward for informers. Further, since it is declared to me that before this persistently cold winter weather the price of grain in the colony was eight or nine *asses* per *modius*, and since it would be the height of iniquity that anyone should make a profit out of the hunger of his fellow-citizens, I forbid the sale price of grain to rise above one *denarius* per *modius*.

[Col. 3] [---] Rufus, imperial procurator.

4. THE PERSONALITY OF THE EMPEROR: CULT AND ACTIVITY
(see also 14, 19, 71, 77, 87, 136, 161, 207)

By the time Tiberius became emperor in 14 the 'imperial cult' had taken root in East and West. Formal deification of Augustus on his death gave it a new impetus, and a new function: to enhance the legitimacy of a successor. Tiberius was son of a god ('Divi filius'), so were Nero, Titus and Domitian, Trajan and Hadrian.

165 Pliny, *Panegyric* 11.1–2. The being (Nerva) whom you (Trajan) first mourned as a son should, you proceeded to honour with temples. You were not imitating those who did the same, but with quite different intentions. Tiberius consecrated Augustus to heaven, but with the purpose of introducing the charge of diminishing the majesty of the Roman People, and Nero consecrated Claudius just to make fun of him. Titus consecrated Vespasian, Domitian Titus, but the first did so with the object of appearing as the son of a god, the second of appearing as brother of one. [2] You gave your father a position amongst the stars, not to frighten your fellow-citizens, insult the gods, or extol yourself, but because you believed him to be a god.

In 14 provincials were uncertain whether the new emperor would require a duplicate of existing institutions and buildings or identical honours. Tiberius distinguished himself from Augustus, but was hard put to refuse well-meant honours when acceptance gave the proposers hope that their own future requests would be taken seriously. The inscription from Gytheion in the Peloponnese leaves it unclear whether the honours Tiberius deprecated were put into effect or not.

166 EJ² 92. March–June 15. Greek. [--- (?the magistrate in charge of the market)] is to set on it [--- on the ?first pedestal an image of the deified Augustus Caesar] the father, on the [second] from the right one of [Julia Augusta], on the third, one of Tiberius Caesar Augustus; [the] images are to be provided for him by the city. [And] a table is also to be set out by him in the centre of the theatre, and an incense burner placed upon it and members of the council and all the authorities are to offer sacrifice [upon it] for the welfare of our leaders, before the entry of the performers.

He is to devote the first day to the deified Augustus, son of the deified Caesar, saviour and liberator, the second to Emperor Tiberius Caesar, Augustus and Father of the Fatherland, the third to Julia Augusta, the Good Fortune of our league and city, the fourth to the Victory of Germanicus Caesar, the fifth to the Aphrodite of Drusus Caesar, the sixth to Titus Quinctius Flamininus; and he is to be responsible for the orderly conduct of the contestants.

He is to render account to the city for the entire cost of hiring the performers and of the administration of the sacred funds at the first assembly after the games; and if he is found on enquiry to have misappropriated funds or to have falsified his accounts he is to be banned from all further office and his property is to be confiscated to the people ... The magistrate in charge of the market, after completing the days of theatrical performances devoted to the gods and leaders, is to bring the performers on to the stage for two further days, one devoted to the memory of Gaius Julius Eurycles, who was an outstanding benefactor of the league and the city, and the second in honour of Gaius Julius Laco, who is the present guarantor of the defence and security of our league and city. He is to hold the performance starting on the day of the goddess on such days as he is able; and when he goes out of office he is to hand over to the magistrate in charge of the market who succeeds him a list drawn up for public use of requisites for the performance, and the city is to receive a copy from the man who takes it over.

Whenever the magistrate in charge of the market holds the theatrical performances he is to conduct a procession from the temple of Asclepius and Hygieia which is to be accompanied by the young men in training, the younger members of the citizen body, and the rest of the citizens, wearing wreaths of laurel and dressed in white. The sacred virgins and the married women are also to join in the procession, wearing sacral dress. When the procession arrives at the shrine of Caesar the overseers are to sacrifice a bull for the safety of the leaders and gods and for the continuation of their rule for ever, and when they have sacrificed they are to constrain the communal messes and their fellow-magistrates to sacrifice in the market place. If they fail to secure that the procession takes place, or do not sacrifice, or if when they have sacrificed they fail to constrain the communal messes and their fellow-magistrates to sacrifice in the market place, they are to pay the gods a sacred fine of 2,000 drachmas ... Terentius Bias and his fellow-overseers in office with Chaeron, general and priest of the deified Augustus, are to contribute three carved representations of the deified Augustus and Julia Augusta and Tiberius Caesar Augustus and the benches in the theatre for the chorus and four doors for the stage performances and a platform for the musicians. They are also to set up a stone plinth, inscribing the sacred law on it, and are to deposit in the public archives a copy of the sacred law, so that being placed both in a public place and in the open and where it is visible to all, the law may display for all men to see how [enduring] is the thankfulness of the people of Gytheion to the rulers. But if they do not inscribe this law or set up the plinth in front of the temple or write out the copy [---].

[Letter of Tiber]ius. [Tiberius Caesar] Augustus son of [the deified Augustus], Supreme Pontiff, [in the sixteenth year] of his tribunician power, sends greetings to the overseers of Gytheion and to the city. Decimus Turranius Nicanor, the envoy sent by you [to] me and to my mother, has delivered to me your letter, to which has been appended the legislation passed [by you] providing for the homage to my father, honour to ourselves. I thank you for them; but my understanding is that what is fitting for all mankind in general and your city in this particular case is to keep in reserve choice honours suitable to the greatness of the benefits conferred by my father on the whole world; I myself am satisfied with those more modest and suitable for a mortal man. My mother, however, will send you an answer when she hears from you what your decision is concerning the honours offered to her.

Personal appearances by popular members of the imperial family could generate enormous enthusiasm – which presumably was expected to elicit fresh signs of favour, in this case from Germanicus Caesar.

167 EJ² 379. Greek papyrus. 18–19. The magistrate: 'I have given both the decrees to the Imperator himself.' The Imperator: 'I, sent by my father, men of Alexandria [---].' The crowd shouted: 'Hooray! Lord, good luck! You will get blessings!' The Imperator: 'You set great store, men of Alexandria, on my talking with you; hold on until the time when I finish the answer to each of your questions, then make your feelings clear. Sent, as I said, by my father to settle the overseas provinces, I have an extremely hard commission. First there is the voyage and being dragged away from my father and grandmother, mother, brother and sister, my children and close friends. The command in front of me [---] the house [---] that there is a new sea, first that I may gaze on our city.' The crowd shouted: 'Good luck!' The Imperator: 'Even before, I considered it was the most brilliant sight, first of all because of the hero and founder, to whom there is a kind of common debt on the part of those who have the same ideals, and then because of the benefits of my grandfather Augustus and of my father [---] demands in my opinion right towards me and further I say nothing.' The crowd shouted: 'Hooray! Extra long life to you!' The Imperator said: 'What each of you knows, I remembered and I found these things multiplied, treasured up in your prayers. For decrees have been written down to do us honour even when a few men have been gathered together [---]'

Germanicus responded cautiously in an edict to Alexandrian enthusiasm.

168 EJ² 320(b). Greek papyrus. 19. Germanicus Caesar, son of Augustus, grandson of the deified Augustus, proconsul, speaks as follows: Your goodwill, which you always show whenever you see me, I accept; but I thoroughly deprecate your expressions, which are invidious to me and appropriate for the gods. For they are fitting only for the person who is truly the saviour and benefactor of the entire race of human beings, my father and his mother, who is also my grandmother. The honours that are reasonable for us (?) are secondary in comparison with their divinity, so that if you do not pay attention to me you force me to make my appearances among you infrequent.

Precedent was relevant, and Tiberius accepted a temple from the Commune of Asia after he had helped defend the province from extortion; senate and Livia were included in the cult (Tacitus, *Ann.* 4.15.4–5). But in territory without a province-wide imperial cult, such as Baetica, Tiberius was unwilling to make concessions (Tacitus, *Ann.* 4.37–8). Gaius Caligula, who came into his power at twenty-five and was keen to explore its limits, was not so scrupulous. His plan to have his statue set up in the Temple at Jerusalem (allegedly in response to accusations brought against Alexandrian Jews) was an experiment doomed to lead to disaster.

169 Josephus, *Jewish Antiquities* 18.261, 263, 269–70, 273–5, 303–5. Gaius resented being so gravely and exceptionally slighted by Jews, and sent Petronius to Syria to take over the office held by Vitellius. He instructed Petronius to enter Judaea with a strong force, and, if the Jews welcomed him, to set up his statue in the temple of God; if they were obdurate, he was to put them down by force and then put up the statue ... |263| But many tens of thousands of Jews presented themselves to Petronius at Ptolemais to petition him not to force them into anything that was lawless or broke their traditional code ... |269| And Petronius saw from what they said that their spirit was unconquerable and that it would not be without a battle that he would be able to manage the erection of the statue for Gaius: there would be rivers of blood. He picked up his friends and the court he had in attendance on him, and pressed on to Tiberias with the purpose of noting how things were with the Jews there ... |270| Again many tens of thousands confronted Petronius when he was at Tiberias and went on their knees to him not by any means to impose such constraints on them and not to pollute the city by putting up statues ... |273| This was the moment when Aristobulus, brother of King Agrippa, and Helcias the Elder, and the other most important members of this dynasty, along with the most prominent Jews, presented themselves before Petronius and called on him not to do anything that would drive the ordinary people to frenzy; he saw how roused they were. |274| He should write to Gaius of their irremediable antagonism against accepting the statue ... |275| It might be that Gaius' resolution would break and that he would not take any savage course of action, or resolve on destroying the Jewish people ...

|303| And (Gaius) was tortured by the trial of his authority that people had dared to make ... He wrote to Petronius: |304| 'Since you have rated such gifts as the Jews have offered you higher than my instructions, and have been puffed up enough to run everything at their pleasure, infringing my instructions, I bid you become your own judge; consider what you ought to do in your own case, since you have brought my anger on yourself ... ' |305|. This was the letter he wrote Petronius; not that Petronius received it while Gaius was still alive: the ship carrying the messengers with it was so delayed that letters bearing the news of Gaius' death reached him first.

As an emperor keen on his own open elevation to a status higher than human, Domitian, like Caligula, was ill regarded. (Cf. Suetonius, *Domitian* 13.)

170 Dio 67.5.7. For he was already demanding to be thought of as a god, and took an inordinate pleasure in being called 'master' and 'god'; these terms were used not only orally but in documents too.

Claudius' position demanded that he impose cult on the Britons, with a vast altar at the centre, just as Augustus had imposed it on the Gauls: a focus of loyalty and something to give well-off subjects of the northern provinces a means of identifying themselves with the ruling power (see Section 3.5 above).

Claudius was cautious and modest-sounding, as Tiberius had been, even in Egypt, but the principle of accepting honours in return for benefactions made him clearer in expressing his wishes than Tiberius had been (LACTOR 8, 27): he simply drew up a list of the honours he would accept and those he would not; after that follows the list of Alexandrian requests that he would allow, and those he would not.

In provinces such as Asia where the cult had been established from the beginning of the Principate, cities vied with each other for the honour of being selected as Temple-Warden (*neocorus*) of the cults established for each new emperor.

171   MW 142. From Ephesus. Towards the end of Domitian's reign. Greek.   For Ephesian Artemis and Emperor [Domitian] Caesar Augustus [Germanicus] the city of the Ephesians, Temple-Warden, established from its own resources the paving of the Enbolos; Marcus Atilius Postumus Bradua the proconsul consecrated it, with Marcus Tigellius Lupus Philocaesar, Secretary to the People, negotiating the business and bringing it to completion.

With the fall of Augustus' dynasty and the establishment of a new one of undistinguished origins, additional efforts had to be made. Pliny the Elder stresses a commonplace idea, since helpfulness was Vespasian's only claim to divinity.

172   Pliny, *Natural History* 2.17–19.   But it is beyond every form of impudence that adulterous acts should be imagined as taking place between the very gods, leading to quarrelling and feuds, and that they should actually be gods of theft and crimes. |18| It is 'god' when one mortal human being helps another, and this is the way to everlasting glory: this is the way that Roman leaders took, the way that the mightiest ruler of any age, Vespasian Augustus, is following, his tread heaven-bound, along with his offspring, as he comes to the rescue of our worn-out state. |19| This is the most ancient method of acknowledging gratitude for good deeds, to enroll men like this among the gods.

Dio of Prusa, addressing Trajan, taught the same lesson.

173   Dio of Prusa, Discourse 3, *On Kingship*, 123–7.   He is the only man who has come to think of happiness, not as comfort, but much rather as excellence of character; merit as something not imposed but as a matter of choice; endurance not a question of hardship but of security; and he enhances his pleasures by his hard work, and derives more benefit from them because of it, while he lightens the hard work by being accustomed to it. |124| In his view 'useful' and 'pleasing' are equivalents: he sees private citizens, if they have any prospect of staying healthy and surviving into old age, never plying an inert and lazy body with food. He see them working previously at trades, some of them very exhausting: smiths, for instance, shipbuilders, and construction workers. |125| Those who have come into landed property first work at farming, while city dwellers are busy with city affairs of some kind. |126| Some are men of leisure; the gymnasia and wrestling schools are full of them; and he sees them running on the tracks, or again wrestling, while others, who are not athletes, he sees doing something else not connected with competing. In short, he sees everyone who is not a complete fool practising something and enjoying food and drink that do them good. [127] But the ruler is different from all these: he doesn't work in vain or develop only his physique: his aim is to get something done. Either he has come to something that needs foresight, or he has anticipated when the need is for speed, or achieved something not easy to achieve, or he has disposed his troops, subdued some territory, or founded a city, bridged rivers, or made a country passable with his roads.

Yet there were important developments in the imperial cult under the Flavians. It spread to new provinces and became consolidated, embracing the cult of the previously deified emperors, and bringing Vespasian and his sons within the fold. The view has prevailed that Vespasian took the initiative in extending the cult to Narbonensis, Baetica, Africa and other provinces. Rather, perhaps, provinces that had found themselves backing other candidates in the Year of the Four Emperors decided to ingratiate themselves with Vespasian on his success, and he acquiesced. This would be parallel with the initiative of Asia and Bithynia in 29 BC after Octavian's victory over Antony.

174 Dio 51.20.6. Meanwhile Caesar, amongst his other activities, also gave permission for precincts to be constructed in Ephesus and Nicaea to Rome and his father Caesar, under the name of the Deified Julius. (Ephesus and Nicaea had come to be the leading cities of Asia and Bithynia.) Octavian told the Romans resident there to do honour to these two deities; as to the non-citizens, whom he called 'Greeks', he permitted them to make precincts for himself, the Asians in Pergamum, the Bithynians in Nicomedia.

Rules of the cult established, probably under Vespasian, at Narbo.

175 MW 128, bronze tablet from Narbo. [Honours due to the high priest --- at Na]rbo[--- When the high priest performs the rites] and [sacrifices], the lictors [who attend on magistrates are to attend on him. --- According to the law] and right of [---] the province he [is to have the right of giving his opinion and voting] among the members of the council or senate; likewise [--- he is to have] the right of viewing [public games of the province] from the front seats [among members of the council] or senators [--- . The wife] of the high priest, clad in white or purple garments [on festal days ---] nor is she to take oath against her will or [touch] the body of a dead person nor [--- unless] it is of a person [related to her]. And [it is to be permitted] for her [to be present ---] at public shows in that [province].
  Honours due to one who [has been] high priest. If a man who [has been] high priest has done nothing in breach of this law, then the incumbent high priest [is to ensure --- that --- by ballot] and under oath they decree and make it their pleasure that a man who has vacated the high priesthood should be permitted [to set up] a statue [of himself. The man to whom they have so decreed that he has the right of setting up a statue] and [of inscribing] his own name and that of his father, his place of origin and the year of his high priesthood is to have the right of setting up the statue [at Narbo] within the confines of the temple, unless

Emperor [Caesar ?Vespasian Augustus has accorded someone else the right. And he] is to have the right in his city council place and in the provincial council of Narbonensis of giving his opinion and voting among [men] of his rank according to the law [---]; likewise, when a public show [is given] in the province, of [attending among members of the council] in a magistrate's toga, and on those days on which he made sacrifices when he was high priest [of wearing in public] the dress [which he wore when making them].

Possible lack of high priest in the community. If there ceases to be a high priest in the community and no substitute has been elected for him then as each [high priest --- is at Narbo] within three days of his being informed and being able he is to perform the rites at Narbo and is to conduct [all those rites throughout the rest] of the year [according to the law] in the order in which [the rites] of the annual high priest [are conducted, and if he conducts them for not less than thirty days] the same law, right and claims are to apply [to him] as apply to one [who has been elected] high priest of Augustus [according to the prescription of this law].

Place in which the [provincial] council is to be held. Those who assemble for the provincial council in Narbo are to hold it there. If any business is transacted at a council held outside Narbo or the boundaries of the people of Narbo it [is not to be held] lawful and valid.

Money [earmarked for rites]. A man who has vacated the high priesthood is to use [the surplus] of the money [which has been earmarked for the rites, to dedicate] statues and images of Emperor Caesar [?Vespasian Augustus] within the said temple [at the discretion of the] incumbent governor of the province [--- And he is to prove] before the official who [computes the finances of the province that he has] in this respect done [everything as provided in this law ---] temple [---]

The Divine House (*Domus Divina*) consisting of all members of the imperial family, whose divinity was derived from that of the emperor, was now a well-established phenomenon, having appeared in Spain under Tiberius and in Britain under Claudius. (For later occurrences, see **189, 204, 238** below.)

176 Sm. *G–N* 197. Noviomagus, Chichester, Britain.   The temple was dedicated to Neptune and Minerva for the welfare of the Divine House on the authority of Tiberius Claudius Cogidubnus, High King of Britain, by the guild of smiths and its members out of their own resources, [---]ens the son of Pudentinus providing the site from his own purse.

The 'Augustan House' was already receiving official acknowledgement by 19, as is shown by the senatorial decrees connected with the honours paid to Germanicus (*Tabula Siarensis*) and with the trial of his alleged murderer (the Senatorial Decree on Cn. Piso the Elder).

177 *Tabula Siarensis* 1.10–11.   It pleased the senate that an arch made of marble should be constructed in the Circus Flaminius at [public] expense, sited at that place in which statues to the Deified Augustus and the Augustan House had been constructed by Gaius Norbanus Flaccus.

Senatorial Decree on Cn. Piso the Elder.

178 *SC de Cn. Pisone patre.* **159–61.** Further, the senate approves the loyalty of those soldiers, whose temper was vainly tried by the crime of Cn. Piso the Elder, and hopes that all those who are our soldiers under the auspices and command of our Leader, will invariably show the loyalty and devotion to the Augustan House that they have shown, since they are aware that the safety of our Empire has been placed in the charge of that House.

The cult benefited the emperor and his family; the wealthy who provided festivals, enhancing their position in their own communities and in the provincial assemblies that organised province-wide cult; and the people who attended and ate meat left over from sacrifices enjoyed the buildings that their city was given, and shared its enhanced importance and beauty. A powerful dynast of Attaleia in Pamphylia, a leading centurion and entrusted with reconstruction at Cyrene in 117, was high priest of all the Augusti.

179 **Sm.** *N–H* **313.** Lucius Gavius Fronto, son of Lucius Gavius Fronto, leading centurion of the Third, Cyrenaican, Legion, and Prefect of the camp of the Fifteenth, Apollinaris, Legion, the first and only one from his native city; father of Lucius Gavius Aelianus, quaestor and propraetor of the Roman people, grandfather of Lucius Gavius Clarus, possessor of the broad striped tunic; honoured by Augustus with the public horse and marks of distinction; entrusted by the deified Trajan with three thousand legionary veterans for the settlement of Cyrene; first to be proclaimed holder of the perpetual quinquennial gymnasiarchy, high priest of all the Augusti for a four-year period and producer from his own resources of scenic and athletic games: Lucius Gavius Seleucus, to his own patron and benefactor.

When there was not enough money to provide for cult without discomfort it was a source of discontent (see Section 3.5 above). Naturally, too, local rivalries focused on the cult, within as well as between cities, as a weapon against political enemies: Dio of Prusa 43.11–12 (**121** above; cf. Pliny, *Ep.* 10.81–2).

To question the 'sincerity' behind the cult is misplaced. Genuine affection, gratitude and pride will also have reinforced conventional attitudes: LACTOR 8, 100, was dedicated to the deified Trajan after his death by the community of Artispi in Spain, and attests enthusiasm for him in his native province.

Even without cult the exchange of homage for received imperial benefits was a powerful binding factor in the Empire.

180 **EJ² 319. Aezani, Phrygia, Asia. Not long after 4. Greek.** Letter [of Tiberius Caesar brought from] Bononia in Gaul. Tiberius Caesar [sends greetings] to the [council] and people of the Aezanitans. Having been acquainted from the beginning with your [respect] and fellow-feeling towards me, I have had great pleasure now too in receiving from your ambassadors [the decree which] demonstrates the goodwill of the city [towards me]. I shall try, [then], to join in assisting {you} to the best of my ability on all occasions on which you claim to receive my help.

A century later the philhellene young relative of Trajan exchanged honours with the city of Athens by holding its archonship in 112.

181 Sm. *N–H* 109. In the theatre of Dionysus, Athens. Last two lines in Greek.
To Publius Aelius Hadrianus, son of Publius, of the Sergian tribe, consul, member
of the seven-man board for the management of feasts, member of the sodality of
Augustales, legate of praetorian rank of Nerva Trajan Caesar Augustus
Germanicus Dacicus of Pannonia Inferior, praetor, and at the same time legate
of the First, Minervian, Legion, devoted and loyal, in the Dacian War; likewise
tribune of the plebs, quaestor of Emperor Trajan and member of his suite on
the Dacian expedition, twice awarded military decorations by him, tribune of
the Second, Auxiliary, Legion, devoted and loyal, likewise of the Fifth,
Macedonian, Legion, likewise of the Twenty-second, Primigenia, Legion,
devoted and loyal, member of the six-man group of the squadron of Roman
cavalry, prefect in charge of the Latin Festival, member of the ten-man board in
charge of judging cases.
   The Council of the Areopagus and that of the Six Hundred and the People of
Athens honour their Archon Hadrian.

Whatever their views, provincials were expected to take oaths of loyalty to a new
emperor.

182 Sm. *G–N* 32. Bronze tablet from Aritium, Lusitania. 37.   Under Gaius
Ummidius Durmius Quadratus, praetorian legate of Gaius Caesar Germanicus,
hailed Imperator. Oath of the people of Aritium: It is my heartfelt intention to be
a personal enemy of whomsoever I discover to be enemies of Gaius Caesar
Germanicus, and if anyone causes or shall cause any danger to him or his security,
I shall not cease to pursue him with the sword and relentless war by land and sea
until he has paid the penalty to Caesar; nor shall I hold myself or my children
dearer than his safety, and those of hostile mind to him I shall consider to be
enemies to me.
   If I knowingly forswear myself or break my oath in future, then may Jupiter
Best and Greatest and the deified Augustus and all the rest of the immortal gods
make me forfeit my native land, my personal safety and all my property.
   11 May in the township of Old Aritium in the consulships of Gnaeus
Acerronius Proculus and Gaius Petronius Pontinus Nigrinus, the officers in
charge being Vegethus son of Tallicus and [...]ibius son of [...]arionus.

5. THE IMPACT OF HER PROVINCES ON ROME

5.1 Manpower: the army and political life

It was some months before Trajan visited Rome after his accession. The court was with
him and he could issue his decisions from wherever he was. Hadrian spent much of
his reign touring the provinces. The time would come when emperors (admittedly
short-lived) would never reach the theoretical seat of government, senate and popular
assemblies. It would be hard to overestimate the importance of Rome's Empire to her:
she had always depended on it for manpower, financial resources and increasingly for

grain, as Josephus makes King Agrippa remind the rebellious Jews in 66, in connexion with north Africa.

183 Josephus, *Jewish War* **2.382–3, 386.** The third part of the inhabited world, of which one would have difficulty even in counting the tribes, which is bounded by the Atlantic Ocean and by the Pillars of Hercules and which supports the Ethiopian hordes up to the Red Sea, this they have taken in hand, all of it; [383] apart from their annual crops, which feed the masses at Rome, they pay tribute of all kinds and readily provide contributions to supply the needs of the Empire. Unlike you, they do not consider anything outrageous in the régime, even though they have a single legion stationed among them … [386] The length of it (Alexandria) is thirty stades, its breadth not less than ten, and it provides in one month more to Rome than you pay in a year; and aside from money four months' grain.

Italy began to fail as a supplier of recruits (Tacitus, *Ann.* 4.4.4). Troops increasingly came from the provinces, both enfranchised provincials admitted to the legions and auxiliary troops, some press-ganged as soon as their region had been conquered (Tacitus, *Ann.* 4.46–51).

Letters of a legionary soldier to his parents.

184 Sm. *N–H* **307(a) and (b). 19 February and 26 March 107. Greek.**
(a) [Apollinarius] to Tasucharion, [my] lady mother, very many greetings. [Before everything] I pray that you are well, which is a [subject of prayer] for me, to embrace you in full health. [*4½ lines fragmentary*] For whenever I remember [you] I don't eat or drink, but cry [*3 lines fragmentary*]. But I thank Serapis and [Good] Fortune that when everyone is working hard all day cutting stones I as a leading ranker am free to move about doing nothing. And I have received pay, and I wanted to send you a present made of Tyrian purple, and on account of [your not] having written back I have[n't] trusted anyone because of the length of the journey. For this is the way fine cloaks and ebony and drinking cups and perfumes are easily brought up. That's why I'm asking [you, my] lady, [---] and to be [-] and cheerful and in good spirits. For that's the good way. For if you two are unhappy it is anguish to me. You will make an effort then to ask a friend of mine at Alexandria so that through him you can send me coarse linen clothing. As it is there is none available and it is very hot. [---] 25 Mecheir.

(b) Julius Apollinarius to Julius Sabinus his sweetest father, many greetings. Before everything I pray that you are well, which is my prayer, [because] I revere you next to the gods. But this has worried me, because, when I have written to you very often [through] Saturninus the standard-bearer, and likewise through Julianus the son of Longinus [and through Dios (*erased*)], you have not yet written back to me about your well-being. But all the same, when you are asked you necessarily must before everything hold to writing to me about the well-being of all of you. But I have often asked Longinus, the man who is taking you my note, to carry you something, and he has refused, saying that he couldn't [take it]. But I want you to know [that] Domitius the master-at-arms took along the basket, in which there was [.....] for you. [I] am getting on [well. After] Serapis

granted [me] the good fortune [of a favourable journey here], when others [---
spend] the whole day stone-cutting and doing [other] things, up to today I haven't
had to put up with any of those things. But [also] when I asked Claudius Severus,
the consular governor, that I should be his secretary, and he said that there was
no place available, 'In the meantime', he said 'I will make you secretary to the
legion with prospects of promotion.' By appointment then I went from the
consular to the administrative office to the position at the side of the consular
legate of the legion and the title adjutant. If you love me, then, you will make an
effort to write to me directly about your welfare and if you care for me send me
linen through Sempronius. For traders are coming daily to us from Pelusium. I
shall make an effort directly if the commander begins to grant leave to come
directly to you all. Volussius Proculus embraces you, (*five others named*), [and]
so do all my messmates. Embrace Julia my lady sister (*and six others*), and all
your colleagues by name and the people at home. I bid you fare well. In the tenth
year of our lord Trajan, 20 Phamenoth. (*PS in margin*) I thank Volussius and
Longinus Barbarus. You will get in touch with the firm of Aphodas, son of the
spice dealer, to tell them that they have posted me to the cohort at Bostra. It is
eight days from Petra and t (*unfinished*)

We are looking at the lower levels of society. Slaves too were still coming from
the provinces, notably cultivated youngsters who might pass into trusted positions in
the imperial entourage itself. Pallas, evidently from the Peloponnese, was in charge of
imperial finances (*a rationibus*) under Claudius and Nero, and remains the most famous
(Tacitus, *Ann.* 12.53). The origins, even the personal name, of another powerful finance
secretary, Tiberius Julius, born about 2 or 3, exiled 82/3, and died late in 92, are
unknown, but he married a distinguished senator's sister, Tettia, and their son received
an address in which his father's position as Tiberius' freedman, serving under Gaius
and Claudius too, was celebrated.

185 Statius, *Silvae* 3.3.66–71, 78–9, 85–96, 115–18.
> Tiberius' court was first to take you in,
> when youth had scarcely touched your cheeks; and there
> your gifts by far outstripped your years, and that
> brought freedom as reward. The nearest heir,
> relentless as he was, and hunted by
> the hounds of hell, still kept you by his side,
> and youth was not a bar to journeying
> with him to northern lands, the frosty Bear's
> domain.
>   ...
[78] And aged Claudius raised you worthily
> to special work, before he went aloft
> to starry heaven.
>   ...
[85] And now a light divine has come into
> your loyal home, and lofty Fortune at
> full stride: for now a single man has charge
> of sacred wealth, the management of gains

from every people, sums the mighty world
demands. What Spain throws forth from golden seams,
the gleaming metal from the Balkan mount,
whatever harvest's swept from Africa,
whatever's threshed by burning Nile, or what
the Red Sea diver spies and takes, the sheep
from rich Tarentine grazing lands, the snows
like glass, Numidian wood, the glorious tusk
that comes from past the Indus, all obey
a single agent, all the North or wild
East Wind bring in, or cloudy South.
...

[115] Etrusca's line was far from mean; the rods
and axes were her brother's, and the chair
of highest office. Faithfully he bore his trust,
Italian swords and standards, when the mad
attack fell on the savage Dacians and
the tribe was doomed to grace a mighty march
of triumph.

We have already seen the army as a means of social advancement. It operated for provincials as well as Italians. The Sicilian Lucius Baebius Juncinus reached the second most senior position in Egypt.

186 Sm. *N–H* 249. From Messina in Sicily. Lucius Baebius Juncinus, son of Lucius, of the Galerian tribe, prefect of Engineers, prefect of the Fourth Cohort of Raetians, military tribune of the Twenty-second, Deiotarian, Legion, prefect of the cavalry squadron of Asturians, prefect in charge of the vehicles belonging to the public post, juridical officer of Egypt.

The opportunities were diverse enough to cater for a variety of talents. Tiberius Julius Alexander, an Alexandrian Jew who had given up his faith for his career, reached the procuratorship of Judaea in the forties (Josephus, *Jewish Antiquities* 20.101–3) and in 66 the governorship of Egypt (LACTOR 8, 50). Gaius Stertinius Xenophon of Cos began with military posts but became Claudius' doctor and was instrumental in securing freedom for his native island in 53; inevitably he was thought to be involved in Claudius' sudden death the following year (Tacitus, *Ann.* 12.61; 67.2).

187 Sm. *G–N* 262. Greek. [Gaius Stertinius] Xenophon, son of Heracleitus, of the Cornelian tribe, head physician to the Deified Augusti and in charge of replies to petitions in Greek; previously military tribune and prefect of engineers, and decorated in the triumph [over] the Britons with a gold crown and a spear; son of the Coan people, lover of [Nero], of the Caesars, of the Augusti, of the Romans, of his native land; benefactor of his fatherland, high priest of the gods and priest for life of the Augusti and of Asclepius and Hygieia and Epione. Set up when Marcus Septicius Rufus, son of Marcus, was temple treasurer, and Ariston the son of Philocles, both lovers of the Caesars.

Individual provincials entered the senate in the second half of the last century BC, notably under Caesar and the Second Triumvirate, in the aftermath of civil wars in which they had served the winning side. Augustus was more discriminating. One striking example is that of Pompeius Macer of Mytilene, Lesbos. His forbear had been Pompey's secretary and biographer, and his father a procurator of Asia. Macer rose to the praetorship in 15 (Tacitus, *Ann.* 1.72.4) but in 33 died with his father-in-law Gaius Julius Laco of Sparta on suspicion of treasonable activity (Tacitus, *Ann.* 6.18.3–5). Their history also illustrates the interconnections between rising families. Laco's enjoyed an intermittent pre-eminence at Sparta, with lapses from favour.

188 Sm. *G–N* 200. Taenarum, Laconia. Greek. The Commune of the Free Laconians (honours) Gaius Julius Laco, son of Eurycles, its own benefactor. Damarmenidas, serving as general, supervised the work.

Compare, in the next generation:

189 Sm. *G–N* 264. Corinth, Achaea. To Gaius Julius Spartiaticus, son of Laco, procurator of Caesar and of Augusta Agrippina, military tribune, honoured by the deified Claudius with the horse provided at public expense, flamen of the deified Julius, pontiff, twice quinquennial duovir, producer of the Isthmian and Caesarian Augustan games, high priest of the Augustan House with unlimited tenure, first man of the Achaeans, on account of his merit and for his keen and superlatively generous munificence towards the divine house and towards our colony. The tribesmen of the Calpurnian Tribe, to their patron.

These interconnexions became even more noticeable in the Flavian and Trajanic period, when C. Julius Severus of Ancyra, Galatia, boasted of his ties.

190 Sm. *N–H* 215. Ancyra, Galatia. Greek. Gaius Julius Severus, descendant of Deiotarus, and of King Amyntas the son of Brigatus, and of Amyntas the son of ?Dyrialus the tetrarchs, and of King Attalus of Asia; cousin of the consulars Julius Quadratus, King Alexander, Julius Aquila and Claudius Severus; kinsman of a very large number of senators; brother of Julius Amyntianus; leading member of the Greek community; he held the high priesthood and excelled in acts of largesse and the other forms of beneficence all who have ever sought honour by that means; during that same year he provided a continuous supply of olive oil in the concourse of the people; he also held office as priest of Augustus and as the first and only priest to make a gift of the resources traditionally belonging to the priesthood for the benefit of the city instead of using the fund for olive oil [as] all his predecessors had done; he also held the offices of archon, producer of games and market supervisor, and made his wife a high priestess who likewise was remarkable for her acts of largesse; he entertained the armies that were wintering in the city and escorted on their way those that were passing through to the war against the Parthians; he lives a life of justice and equity, and the tribe Paraca[---], the seventh, under the tribal presidency of Varus Logius, did honour to their benefactor.

In the East, men of affluent cities of the province of Asia were favoured with advancement; in the West, it was citizens of such Spanish colonies and municipalities as Corduba (Seneca and members of his family, including Lucan) and Italica (the father of Trajan, the first emperor of provincial origin), and the landed native magnates of Narbonensian Gaul. Claudius in 48 began extending to northern Gallic tribes the right to wear the broad stripe on the tunic in token of their intention to stand for senatorial office (LACTOR 8, 34; cf. Tacitus, *Ann.* 11.23–5).

Under Trajan a ruling that candidates for senatorial office must deposit one third of their cash capital in Italian land met with senatorial approval, on the face of it because the provincial senators would no longer be fly-by-night opportunists but have a stake in the land (Pliny, *Ep.* 6.19). It was not only their money that Rome wanted. Many of the men admitted were talented (cf. Tacitus, *Hist.* 2.81) and knew that they had to please to get on; a post burdensome to an Italian could give them just the kudos that they needed. The career of Gnaeus Julius Agricola illustrates the ideal of hard work and loyalty.

Reconstruction of senatorial and equestrian orders after the Year of the Four Emperors began with the admission of new senators as Vespasian took power; it culminated in his and Titus' censorship of 73–4.

191 ***RIC* 2, 34, no. 165:** *aureus* **from Rome, 73.** *Obverse.* Head of Titus, laureate, right. TITUS CAESAR IMPERATOR VESPASIAN, PONTIFF, (with) TRIBUNICIAN POWER, CENSOR.
Reverse. Victory advancing, right, holding wreath and palm. VICTORY OF AUGUSTUS

Vespasian admitted the forbears of the Trajanic, Hadrianic and Antonine aristocracy, indeed of the Antonine emperors, still especially from Italy, Spain, Narbonese Gaul and Asia (for Julius Quadratus Bassus, who died on campaign in Dacia, see LACTOR 8, 87); men already in the senate, distinguished soldiers, were admitted to the highest aristocracy by being given patrician status; for the career of one such, Trajan's father, see **51** above.

The circle widened; the reign of Titus saw 'the first consul to come from Africa' (LACTOR 8, 62); but senators from Greek-speaking provinces were especially keen, it seems.

192 Plutarch, *On Peace of Mind* **10 (***Moralia* **470c).** But there is a different type of person, a Chian, or a Galatian or Bithynian, who is not content if he has won the glory or power that goes with a certain position among his fellow-citizens; he is in tears because he does not wear the shoes of a patrician senator; if he does wear them, because he is not yet a Roman praetor; if he is a praetor, because he is not consul; and when he is consul, because he was not the first to be declared elected, but came in later.

Cornutus Tertullus of Perge in Pamphylia, Pliny's friend (e.g. *Ep.* 5.14) and colleague in a suffect consulship of 100, shows senators from Greek-speaking provinces beginning to serve in western provinces and performing military functions there (though Tertullus had Italian ancestry).

193 MW 321. Near Labicum, Latium. To Gaius Julius Cornutus Tertullus, son of Publius, of the Horatia tribe, consul, proconsul of the province of [Asia], proconsul of the province of Narbonensis, legate with praetorian rank of the deified Trajan [Parthicus] of the province of Pontus and Bithynia, legate of the same with praetorian rank of the province of Aquitania, in charge of taking the census, curator of the Aemilian [road], prefect of the treasury of Saturn, legate with praetorian rank of the province of Crete and Cyrene, promoted to praetorian rank by the deified Vespasian and Titus during their censorship, aedile of Ceres, urban quaestor. In accordance with his will, Gaius Julius Plancius Varus Cornutus [---]

The merits of royalties dismissed from client kingdoms may not have been obvious, but Julius Epiphanes Philopappus of Commagene reached the consulship in 109 and still attracts attention with his lofty monument next to the Acropolis at Athens; the inscription honouring him there brings out his dual identity as Roman senator and member of a dynastic family.

194 Sm. *N–H* 207. Athens. Bilingual.   (*Latin*) Gaius Julius Antiochus Philopappus, son of Gaius, of the Fabian tribe, consul, member of the Arval brotherhood, co-opted into the ranks of the ex-praetors by Emperor Caesar Nerva Trajan Optimus Augustus Germanicus Dacicus. (*Greek*) King Antiochus Philopappus son of King Antiochus Epiphanes.

Very little merit was seen in Trajan's general Quietus the Moor.

195 Dio 68.32.4.   Lusius Quietus was a Moor, a chieftain of the Moors in his own right, and held the post of commander of a troop of cavalry. But being condemned for unbecoming conduct he was dismissed the army in disgrace. Later, when the Dacian war was imminent and Trajan needed the co-operation of the Moors, he went to Trajan of his own accord and performed great services. He was honoured for this and in the second war achieved even more, and finally in this (Parthian) war got so far as a result of his courage and good luck that he was enrolled in the ranks of the ex-praetors, held the consulship, and governed Judaea. This presumably was the cause of intense jealousy and hatred, and of his death.

5.2 Culture

The acquisition and possession of empire had a profound effect on Roman intellectual life. Roman conquests were summed up and symbolised by the creation of maps such as Agrippa's and by the accumulation of collections, physical and literary: Pliny's universal *Natural History* mirrored the power that Rome enjoyed over the entire world.

196 Pliny, *Natural History*, Preface 16.   For my part I feel that all those who have preferred the usefulness of helping by overcoming difficulties to the influence won by giving pleasure, have a special case to be made for them in scholarship; I myself have already said this in other works as well, and do admit to wondering at Titus Livy, the supremely famous author, when he starts one book of his *Histories*, which he took from the beginning of the city, by saying that 'he had won enough glory, and could have taken a rest, if his restless mind did not feed on work'. Certainly he ought to have written that history for the glory of the people that has conquered the world, and the Roman name, not for his own. He would have done a greater service if he had gone on for love of the work, and offered it to the Roman people, not to himself.

Tacitus, *Ann.* 3.55, noted a change in culture and manners under the Flavians: economy, self-restraint and plainness became the fashion; in Pliny, *Ep.* 7.24, of *c.* 107, notes the different life-styles of the deceased near-octogenarian sybarite Ummidia Quadratilla and her austere grandson. Tacitus and Pliny are writing about upper class Italy, and Tacitus attributes the change to the influx of men into the governing class who came from the country towns of Italy and the provinces; but changes were overtaking the provinces too.

Attempts to demonstrate an individual contribution to the Roman intellectual scene, to find ethnicity in the works of 'Spanish' authors such as the younger Seneca, his nephew Lucan, and Martial have not convinced. Western élites were thoroughly trained in Roman literature and rhetoric.

The encroachments of 'the Greek Renaissance' are very plain to see. Greek speakers entered the senate; philosophers were intimate with the highest ranks of the Roman aristocracy: Stoic and Cynic philosophers proper flourished at Rome during this period, especially in the company and houses of men who were bolstering their political beliefs about the relations of senate and Princeps with philosophical principles. These Greek-speaking gurus suffered expulsion from Rome and Italy more than once, notably in 93. The equestrian Stoic Gaius Musonius Rufus married his daughter to the Syrian guru Artemidorus, whom Pliny held in high esteem (Pliny, *Ep.* 3.11). Upper class Romans sat at the feet of Musonius' pupil, the freedman Epictetus of Hierapolis in Phrygia, and the consular Arrian published his *Discourses*.

197 Epictetus, *Encheiridion* 19. You can be unconquerable if you enter no contest that is not in your power to win. Take care in case some time, when you see someone given more honourable treatment than yourself or in a position of great power or in high repute in some other way, you are carried away by outward appearances and call him blest. For if the essence of Good is included in the things that are within our power, neither envy nor jealousy has any place, and you yourself will not wish to be a praetor or a senator or a consul, but a free man. The sole route that leads to this is despising what is not in our power.

Epaphroditus was another freedman highly esteemed.

198 Suidas, *Lexicon*, 'Epaphroditus' (ed. A. Adler, vol. 2, Leipzig, 1931). Epaphroditus of Chaeroneia, fostered and educated by Archias of Alexandria, was bought by Modestus, the Prefect of Egypt, and taught his son Petelius in Rome. He was prominent under Nero and up to the reign of Nerva, in the same period as Ptolemy, son of Hephaestion, and many others well known in cultural life. He was a persistent buyer of books and collected thirty thousand volumes, serious and recondite, too. In physical appearance he was massive and dark, like an elephant. He lived in the Phaenianokoria district, as it is called, having bought two houses there. When he was in his seventy-fifth year he died, falling ill with dropsy. He left a fair number of written compositions.

The most famous native of Chaeroneia, however, was Lucius Mestrius Plutarch, philosopher, friend of cultivated Romans, Boeotia's representative on the Amphictyonic Council of Delphi, awarded the decorations of an ex-consul, eventually procurator of Achaea. He embodies the cultural coming together of Greece and Rome, and so do his *Parallel Lives* of great Greeks and Romans. He presents his friend Philippus attacking a pretentious Roman dining custom.

199 Plutarch, *Table Talk* **8.1.1 – 2.1 (***Moralia* **711A–B).** What recitals should particularly be used at dinner? Participants: Plutarch, Diogenianus of Pergamum, a sophist, Philippus of Prusa (Stoic).

After this, I prevented the sophist from taking up the argument again. 'One would rather consider this, Diogenianus', I said, 'what type of recital, of the many that there are, would fit best with drinking. Let us invite the wise man here to decide for us' ... [1.2] When therefore both Diogenianus and I invited him, without any demur at all the sophist said that he relegated everything else to the orchestral stage and its altar, but went along with the custom newly introduced into Roman drinking parties, though it had not yet become the rage among ordinary people. [1.3] 'You know', he said, 'that some of Plato's dialogues are in narrative form, others dramatic. Slave boys are learning the sprightliest of these dramatic ones, so as to give recitals of them from memory. They also have a delivery suitable to the characters being represented, the voice and gesture are inflected, and the expression goes along with what is being said ... [1.4] No-nonsense people of taste have become exceedingly fond of this; effeminates and those whose ears are enfeebled because of their ignorance of the arts and who have no experience of the beautiful and who, as Aristoxenus says, spit bile whenever they hear something musical, they were for getting rid of them. And I shouldn't be surprised if they do: effeminacy rules!' [2.1] And Philippus, seeing some people becoming rather annoyed, said, 'Stop, sir, and give up abusing us. We are the people who first took offence in Rome when this practice was introduced, and we laid into the people who thought it was acceptable for Plato to be made a pastime to go with wine-drinking and for them to listen to Plato's dialogues amid sweets and scents.'

The world-wide aristocracy of sophists, well-off intellectuals, educated, articulate and ready to teach, exercised influence at local and sometimes governmental level. The 'Second Sophistic', as Philostratus dubbed the fresh flowering of an interest in dialectic, debate and public speaking that had been practised by sophists, 'professors of wisdom', in Greece of the fifth century BC, flourished from the reign of Vespasian until the third century, a period of self-confidence and prosperity for the Greek cities, especially of Asia; it remains elusive because the essence of it was technique, employed to persuade or entertain.

200 Philostratus, *Lives of the Sophists* **481.** The old sophistic, even when putting forward philosophical subjects, used to go through them diffusely and at length, for it discoursed on courage, it discoursed on justice, on heroes and gods and how the form of the universe has taken shape. But the sophistic that came after that, which is not to be called 'new', for it is old, but rather 'second', sketched the poor and the rich, aristocrats and tyrants and the specific themes to which history leads. Gorgias of Leontini was the originator of the older, in Thessaly, and

Aeschines son of Atrometus when he was banished from political life at Athens and was taking part in social life in Caria and Rhodes. While these people handled the themes according to artistic rule, the followers of Gorgias followed their own opinions.

Sophists handed down established culture and used historical themes for their entertainments or illustrations; they were ambassadors and mediators, even between cities and the emperor. Their stress on effective speaking influenced educated men in the West, who had to confront them in government. Speakers such as Dio of Prusa did their best to unite their Greek world under Roman sway; Marcus of Byzantium was particularly successful, ending a feud that had been going on for half a millennium.

201 Philostratus, *Lives of the Sophists* 529–30. When after that Marcus reached Megara (these people were the founders of Byzantium), the Megarians were at loggerheads with the Athenians and had their minds totally on the feud, just as if the placard imposing a ban on them had recently been drawn up, and when the Athenians arrived for the Lesser Pythian Games they would not allow them in. But Marcus came forward in their assembly and so played upon the Megarians that he persuaded them to open up their houses and let the Athenians in among their women and children. [530] The Emperor Hadrian admired him too, when he had come as an envoy representing the Byzantines; he was the most apt of the early emperors to encourage merit.

Emperors showed themselves favourably disposed towards cultural organisations, as letters of Claudius to Dionysiac performers demonstrate.

202 Sm. *G–N* 373(a). Greek papyrus. January 43. [Tiberius Claudius Caesar Augustus Germanicus, Supreme Pontiff], in his second year [of tribunician power], three times consul, hailed Imperator for the fourth time, Supreme Pontiff, greets those crowned with laurel world-wide as victors in the sacred contests of Dionysus and their fellow competitors. The [---] the legal privileges and benefits granted to you by the deified Augustus I preserve. The envoys were Claudius Pho[..]s, Claudius Epagathus, Claudius Dionysius, Claudius Thamyris [---. ---] was written in Rome in the consulships of Tiberius Claudius Caesar Augustus, for the third time and Vitellius for the second time.

203 Sm. *G–N* 373(b). Miletus. 48–9. Greek. Tiberius Claudius Caesar Augustus Germanicus, in his sixth year of tribunician power, four times consul, hailed Imperator for the fifteenth time, Father of the Fatherland, Censor, greets the victors in the sacred contests of Dionysus and the artists. As you recalled my grants in which I preserved the rights given you by the Augusti my predecessors and by the senate, I approve them and shall endeavour to enhance them, seeing that you are loyally disposed towards my house. This was made known to me by my close friend Marcus Valerius Junianus, whom I also commend for his disposition towards you. Farewell.

Vespasian established chairs of rhetoric at Rome and supported teachers and doctors throughout the Empire, though not philosophers, perhaps because they had been hostile to him for returning Greece once more to Roman rule from the freedom that Nero had granted it (Suetonius, *Vesp.* 17–18). Domitian was cautious about them.

204   MW 458. Pergamum. 27 Dec. 74 (Greek); 93–4 (Latin).   [Emperor Caesar Vespasian Augustus, Supreme Pontiff, in his seventh year of tribunician power, hailed Imperator fourteen times, Father of the Fatherland, five times consul, designated consul for the sixth time, censor, says: Since --- (*account of the merits of teachers and doctors*) ---], I order that neither is billeting to be imposed [on them], nor are they to be asked for tax contributions in any way. [But if any of those] under my leadership [shall dare] to outrage or demand security from [or take to court] any of the physicians or teachers or physiotherapists, those guilty of the outrage are to pay to Capitoline Jupiter [ten thousand drachmas]. Whoever does not have the amount, let him be sold up and let the official [in charge of these matters consecrate to the god] without delay whatever fine [he has imposed]. Likewise if they [find him in hiding], let them take him to court wherever they choose, and [let them not be hindered] by anybody. It is [to be permitted] to them also [to hold assemblies] in whatever precincts and temples and [shrines] wherever they choose, as on sacred ground with the right of asylum. [Whoever does them any violence] is to be liable to answer to the Roman people on a charge of [impiety towards] the House of the Augusti. I, Emperor [Caesar Vespasian], signed this and ordered that [it be displayed on] a white board. Published in the sixth year, on the [?] day of the month [Loos, on the Capitol] six days before the first of January.

[Emperor Caesar Domitian, in his thirteenth year of tribunician power, hailed Imperator for the twenty-second time, censor for an unlimited period, Father of the Fatherland], when Aulus Licinius Mucianus and Gavius Priscus were consuls: [The greed of physicians and] teachers I have decided needs the most severe repression. Their skill, which ought [to be passed on to] select [young men of free birth], is being sold in a most outrageous manner to a number of [personal] slaves who have been sent to acquire [the training, not for cultural reasons] but for greater cash profit. [Whoever therefore shall make] a profit [from the training of slaves, he is to have] taken [from him the tax immunity which was granted by my deified father], just as [if he were practising his art in a city that is not his own].

Severe as the tone of this is, Domitian's devotion to literature and education is not to be doubted: the four-yearly Capitoline Games instituted in 86 to celebrate Jupiter (LACTOR 8, 72) had other aspects, education and training in literature and athletics, and represent a philhellenic side of Domitian's principate.

5.3 Religion

Both Augustus and Vespasian noted the need for religious ceremonies to be restored, and along with them the 'peace of the gods' and the security of the people: Vespasian 'preserved the public ceremonies and restored the sacred temples' (LACTOR 8, 57). But a need was felt long before the crisis of 68–9 for untried and therefore more credible divine help. Christianity was preceded by Egyptian and Persian religion, and Judaism proper.

Egyptian rites had long been popular at Rome, but had been suspect, as an episode from the reign of Tiberius shows. (Cf. **209** below and Tacitus, *Annals* 2.85.5.)

205 **Josephus, *Jewish Antiquities* 18.66–73, 77–9.** Paulina was a woman who because of the distinction of her ancestry at Rome and her own practice of virtue was greatly and increasingly esteemed ... [67] Decius Mundus, an eques of high standing at that time, was in love with her ... [68] He could not bear his ill-luck in love and thought it was right to condemn himself to death by starvation. [69] Mundus had a freedwoman of his father's, Ida, who was skilled in wrong-doing of every kind ... [70] ... She did not follow the same track as those who had previously been engaged as agents, because she could see Paulina's complete imperviousness to money. But she knew that Paulina was strongly under the influence of the cult of Isis, and her plan was as follows: [71] She met some of the priests to talk to them and on the basis of strong assurances, of which the most significant was a gift of money, two and a half thousand down, with the same again when the affair had come off, she let them know all about the young man's passion, and told them to make every effort to secure the woman. [72] They were struck with the money and gave their promise. And the oldest of them hurried to Paulina and on being admitted demanded a private interview with her. This was granted, and he said that he had come at the bidding of Anubis; the god had fallen in love with her and was ordering her to come to him. [73] ... So she went to the temple and after dinner, when it was bedtime and the doors inside the temple had been closed by the priest, and the lamps were out of the way, Mundus, who had been hiding there beforehand, had no trouble in having intercourse with her ... [77] Two days after the transaction Mundus met Paulina and said, 'In spite of everything, Paulina, you have both saved me two hundred thousand that you could have added to your household property, and have not failed to carry out the pact for which I offered them to you' ... [78] But when at that moment she came for the first time to realise the outrage, she tore her robe and revealed the dastardly plot to her husband and asked him not to lose the chance of redress. He informed the Emperor about the business. [79] Tiberius carried out a scrupulous investigation by interrogating the priests and he had them crucified, and Ida too, who had been responsible for the disaster and put together everything that led to the outrage on the woman. And he destroyed the temple and ordered the image of Isis to be thrown into the river Tiber.

Egyptian influence was reinforced by the Egyptian base of the Flavian coup, and by an episode at the end of the war of 69, when Domitian escaped from the Capitol disguised as a priest of Isis (Suetonius, *Dom.* 1.1).

206 **MW 190. *Sestertius* of Tarraco.** *Obverse.* Bust of Vespasian, laureate. EMPEROR CAESAR VESPASIAN AUGUSTUS, SUPREME PONTIFF, (with) TRIBUNICIAN POWER, FATHER OF THE FATHERLAND, CONSUL.
  Reverse. Front view of temple of Isis; statue of the goddess visible in inner shrine.

207 **MW 147. Aeclanum, Italy.** To Cantria Longina, daughter of Publius, priestess and celebrant of the deified Julia Pia Augusta and of the mother of the Gods ?of Mount Ida and of Isis the Queen. These monuments she gave to the community on account of the office of her priesthood, and *HS* 50,000. Set up at public expense and by the decree of the councillors.

The cult of Cybele, long established, remained suspect because of the self-castration practised by her Anatolian priests, who came to Rome in numbers.

208 *ILS* 5172. Rome, formerly on the Appian Way near the property of Flavia Domitilla, Domitian's cousin.
O you who worship Cybele, who weep
for Phrygian Attis, when the time allows
and silent night brings Dindyma to quiet,
lament my ashes. Hector is among
them, really Hector; I who lie here in
this grave, am he, a truly Phrygian shade.
Though puny, I am he who carried on
a mighty name, a tiny person full
of many gifts: of getting horses round
the track; of wrestling in the oily gym;
of putting up with jokes; I knew a trick
or two, knew loyalty too. But you I pray
the gods may grant as much as you deserve.
O Domitilla: you who made the patch
I lie in not too small.

Judaism's exclusivity made it a difficult religion for men in public life to embrace; another anecdote of Josephus illustrates the attraction it had for women. (Cf. **205** above and Tacitus, *Annals* 2.85; Claudius also expelled the Jews from Italy: Suetonius, *Div. Claud.* 25.4.)

209 Josephus, *Jewish Antiquities* 18.81–4. There was a Jew, exiled from his own country because he had been charged with breaking certain laws and was afraid of being punished on that account; but he was an all-round good-for-nothing. Well, at that time he was staying in Rome and pretended to expound the wisdom of the laws of Moses. [82] He brought in three men who in every way had the same characteristics as he had. Fulvia, a woman of the aristocracy who was a proselyte in Jewish ways, used to frequent them, and they persuaded her to send gold and purple to the Temple in Jerusalem, and they took these gifts and made use of them for their own expenditure (that was what the begging had been intended for right from the beginning). [83] Saturninus, the husband of Fulvia, informed Tiberius, who was a friend of his, at the instigation of his wife. And Tiberius ordered the whole Jewish population of Rome into banishment. [84] From these the consuls conscripted four thousand people and sent them to the island of Sardinia, but punished a very large number who were unwilling to serve because they were keeping the ancestral law. And these people, on account of the wickedness of four men, were driven out of the city.

Judaising in high places was severely dealt with by Domitian.

210 Dio 67.14.1–3. And in the same year (95) Domitian slaughtered, among many others, Flavius Clemens, who was consul at the time, in spite of the fact that he was his cousin, and had as his wife Flavia Domitilla, who was also Domitian's kinswoman. [14.2] The charge brought against the pair was that of denying the gods, for which others besides who had drifted into Jewish practices were condemned. Some of them were executed, others at best had their property confiscated. Domitilla was only exiled to Pandateria, [14.3] but Domitian killed Glabrio, who had been consul with Trajan. He was accused amongst other things of the same kind as had been attributed to most of the others, of having fought against wild beasts.

Christianity was a worse evil (Tacitus, *Ann.* 15.44): it took up non-Jews of the lowest rank and was as incapable as Judaism of recognising the validity of pagan practice. But in the stratified society of the Roman Empire it bypassed pagan authority through a familiar system of mediators, offering access to the only and all-powerful God in the face of a human uncertainty that philosophers had long tried to allay.

211 Arrian, *Discourses of Epictetus* **4.1.91–8.** This is what travellers do, too, those who are not inclined to take chances. A man has heard that there are robbers on his route. He does not venture on his way by himself, but waits about for a group belonging to an envoy, pro-quaestor or proconsul; he attaches himself to it and goes on his way safely. [1.92] This is what the sensible man does in the world at large. 'Robbery is widespread; so are autocrats, storms, problems, the loss of all that means most to one. [1.93] Where is one to find refuge? How is one to continue on one's way without falling a victim to robbers? What group is one to wait for so as to go on one's way in safety? To whom should one attach oneself? [1.94] To so-and-so the rich man, the consul? And what good does that do me? He too is stripped, groans, grieves. What if my travelling companion himself turns on me and behaves to me like a robber? What shall I do? [1.95] I shall become a friend of Caesar's; nobody will do me any harm when I am of his company. First of all, to become his friend, the number of things I have to do and put up with! The number of times I have to be robbed, and by how many people! And then if I do become his friend, even he is mortal. [1.96] And suppose for some reason he becomes my enemy, wherever had I better retire? To a desert? [1.97] Why, doesn't fever come there? What is to become of me, then? Isn't it possible to find a reliable fellow-traveller, one that one can trust, strong, incapable of treachery?' [1.98] He puts his mind to this and comes to the conclusion that if he attaches himself to God he will get through safely.

By Pliny's time Christianity was well known throughout the Roman world because of the Great Fire of Rome of 64 (Tacitus, *Ann.* 15. 44; Pliny, *Ep.* 10. 96–7). Christian writing of Domitian's time (or possibly earlier), shows that the hostility of the authorities was reciprocated, with reference to Rome's plundering of her Empire.

212 Revelation of St John the Divine 18.4–5, 7–8, 11–13. And I heard another voice from heaven. It said: 'My people, leave her, so that you have no share in her guilty acts and take none of her plagues. [5] Her sins have reached up far enough to touch heaven, and God has taken note of her acts of injustice … [7]

Give her grief and torment to match her self-glorification and riotous living: she
says to herself, "I am sitting here a queen, I am no widow, and I am certainly not
going to know anything of grief." [8] For this her plagues will come all on one
day, death, grief and hunger, and she will burn down in flames: mighty is the
Lord God who has passed judgement on her ... [11] And the world's merchants
will shed tears over her and grieve, because nobody buys their goods any more,
[12] merchandise of gold, silver, high-priced stone, pearls, linen, purple, silk,
scarlet cloth, every form of citron wood, every piece of ivory furniture, or
furniture made from the most precious wood, bronze and marble, [13] cinnamon,
cardamom, incense, myrrh, cedar, wine, olive oil, the finest wheaten flour, grain,
cargoes of pack animals, sheep, horses, travelling carriages, slaves, living human
beings.'

At the same time, Romans were showing their regard for the cults of classical
Greece. Domitian restored the temple at Delphi, and the Amphictyonic League
followed suit with repairs and new buildings. (Cf. *SIG*³ 823A–C.)

213 **SIG³ 821. 84.**   Emperor Caesar Domitian Augustus Germanicus, son of the
deified Vespasian, Supreme Pontiff, in his third year of tribunician power, Father
of the Fatherland, hailed Imperator for the seventh time, having held the
consulship for the tenth time, designated consul for the [eleventh], restored the
temple of Apollo at his own expense.

Plutarch was a link between Delphi and the ruling class at Rome, and appreciated
the material splendour that the site now enjoyed, whatever the state of the oracle itself.

214 **Plutarch, *On the Oracles at Delphi* 29 (*Moralia* 408F–409A).**   As to the
discourse of the prophetess, mathematicians call the shortest line between two
points a straight line; it is the same with her language: it makes no retractions,
circumlocutions, doubling back or ambiguity, but goes straight for the truth. But
as regards credibility, uncertain as it is, subject to scrutiny, up till now it has not
given any evidence against itself, but has filled the oracle with votives and gifts
from foreigners and Greeks and has provided additional adornments in the form
of beautiful ornaments and furniture for the buildings from the Amphictyonic
League. Certainly you yourselves see many additional foundations of buildings
that did not exist before, many restored of those that had fallen into ruin and
destruction. Just as other trees spring up beside those that are flourishing, so
beside Delphi Pylaea is coming into its heyday and flowering along with it. From
the wealth there it is taking on form, plan and an elegant arrangement of shrines,
meeting houses and fountains. In a thousand years before it never had anything
like it.

Plutarch devoted himself to the service of the shrine, and advised an Athenian
friend, Euphanes, to continue his religious work too.

215 **Plutarch, *Old Men in Public Affairs* 17.3–4 (*Moralia* 792F).**   To be sure, you
know that I have been in official service to Pythian Apollo over many celebrations
of his games. But you would not say, 'Enough of your sacrifices, Plutarch, and

of your processions and choruses. You are becoming an old man; now is the time to put aside your garland and to allow old age to be your reason for abandoning the oracle.' [4] And so you mustn't think either that, when you are leader and spokesman in the sacred activities of your city, you ought to give up the honours you pay to Zeus who is the protector of the city and of the market place, after your long and enthusiastic participation in them.

5.4 Costs

Theoretically the Empire paid, and Rome financed further conquests, benefits for her citizens, and the beautification of the City from it. Subjects enjoyed protection in return for taxes (Tacitus, *Hist.* 4.74), exacting though they were (cf. Section 3.5 above). Armies stationed in the provinces absorbed what taxation brought in and few wars were profitable. New sources of revenue, whether from new provinces or from new taxes, were welcome.

There must have been an influx of booty from Britain, and it began to be exploited as soon as possible after the conquest. Some revenue came from natural resources, but grain was important: **216** below, with *RIB* 2,2. 2415/56, where the possibility of excessive extortion of grain is not ruled out. The vessel holds 11.34 litres, not the 9.54 that is equivalent to the 17½ *sextarii* stated on it; but it may have been intended for weekly distributions of grain to troops at 2½ *sextarii* a day.

216 **MW 527. *Modius* from Carvoran, Hadrian's Wall. 90–1.** When Emperor [Domitian] Caesar Augustus Germanicus was consul for the fifteenth time. Tested to 17 1/2 *sextarii*. Weight 38 pounds.

217 **MW 439. Lead pig from near Chester. 74.** Emperor Vespasian Augustus, consul for the fifth time, Titus Imperator, consul for the third time. Lead from the Deceangli, North Wales.

After the civil wars of 68–9 Vespasian was painfully short of money (Suetonius, *Vesp.* 16.3; cf. *Vit.* 13.2). Imperial properties could be sold; there could be economy and stringent taxation.

218 **Dio 65.2.5, 8.2–5.** But Mucianus was taking in money in untold quantities from all sources and gathering them into the public treasury with great alacrity, and bringing the blame for it on himself instead of Vespasian. He used to say that money was always the sinews of government. Accordingly he urged Vespasian too to fund himself from all over the place while he went on with his original policy of collecting cash, amassing huge wealth for the state as well as acquiring huge sums for himself ...

[8.2] In these ways heaven was making Vespasian great, but the Alexandrians by contrast took no pleasure in him; rather they were thoroughly disgruntled, so that they made jokes about him and abused him, not only in private, but publicly too. They had expected to get some significant advantage from him for having been the first to make him emperor; not only did they find nothing, but they were actually having their money exacted. [8.3] In various ways he collected large amounts from them, neglecting no source of revenue, even a casual one, and even if it was something discreditable; he made money out of everything, sacred and profane alike. Many taxes that were obsolete he reintroduced, others still current he increased, and in addition he established new ones. [8.4] He acted in the very same way later in the rest of the Empire and in Italy and Rome itself. The Alexandrians, then, were annoyed with him for these reasons and besides that because he sold the greater part of the Ptolemaic palaces. Amongst the other abusive cries that they were hurling at him was, 'Six obols more you want now!', so that Vespasian, who was the mildest of men, became angry [8.5] and ordered that the six obols should indeed be exacted from each man, and deliberated about punishing them as well. The words themselves trampled him in the mud, and there was something in the broken rhythm and the anapaests that stung him to anger.

There were numerous stories of Vespasian's own venality (Suetonius, *Vesp.* 23.2). The ending of the Jewish revolt of 66–73 brought great booty, which paid for the construction of the Colosseum (**115** above). But the cost of the war, of restoring the substructure of the country, and of maintaining a senatorial governor and a complete legion in garrison at Jerusalem had to be set against it. After 70 Vespasian found a new, Roman, use for the Jewish poll-tax previously paid for the upkeep of the Temple in Jerusalem. The two shekels annually due to the Temple went to the 'Jewish Treasury' (*Fiscus Judaicus*) as one of Vespasian's most notorious new taxes. (Cf. Dio 65.7.2.)

219 Josephus, *Jewish War* 7.216–18.   About the same time Caesar sent to Bassus and to Laberius Maximus, who was the procurator of Judaea, ordering them to lease out all land belonging to the Jews. [217] For he founded no city there, keeping the land in his own control, although to eight hundred men discharged from the army he did exceptionally give a place to settle, called Emmaus, which was thirty stades from Jerusalem. [218] He imposed tribute on the Jews wherever they lived, demanding two drachmas from each person every year to be paid to the Capitol, just as they used formerly to contribute it to the Temple in Jerusalem.

There is epigraphic evidence for its organisation.

220 MW 203. Rome.   To Titus Flavius Euschemon, freedman of Augustus who was secretary for correspondence and likewise procurator in charge of the Jewish poll-tax. Flavia Aphrodisia made the monument for her well-deserving patron and husband.

Brutal enquiries instituted as to whether individuals were liable for the tax shocked Suetonius in his youth (*Dom.* 12.2); they were mitigated by Nerva.

221 Sm. *N–H* 28. *Sestertius* of 96.   *Obverse.* Head of Nerva, wearing laurel wreath; EMPEROR NERVA CAESAR AUGUSTUS, SUPREME PONTIFF, HOLDING [TRIBUNICIAN] POWER, TWICE CONSUL, FATHER OF HIS COUNTRY.
   Reverse. Palm tree. ABOLITION OF MALICIOUS ACCUSATIONS FOR THE BENEFIT OF THE FISCUS JUDAICUS. BY DECREE OF THE SENATE.

A sherd from Apollinopolis Magna in Egypt bears the last in the series of receipts for the tax.

222 Sm. *N–H* 56. 18 May 116. Greek.   Thermathos, slave of Aninios centurion, for the Jewish tax. 19th year of Trajan Optimus, our Lord, three obols. Year 19, 23rd of the month Pachon.

Another significant item for state revenue was the clarification of boundaries. For the state it simplified collection of revenue and for the cities it secured their finances, especially if their public property had been taken over by private individuals and was now recovered, as it was in one Roman colony.

223 MW 447, from Arausio, Narbonensis. 77.   (a) [Emperor] Caesar [Vespasian] Augustus, Supreme Pontiff, in his eighth year of tribunician power, saluted Imperator for the [eighteenth] time, Father of the Fatherland, having held the consulship eight times, censor.
   (b) [For the restoration of sites belonging to the public] which [the Deified Augustus] had given [to the troops of] the Second, Gallic, Legion [which had been in the possession of private individuals] for a number of years
   (c) [He ordered the table] to be displayed in public [with the yearly tax in each [century of land noted down, --- overseeing the proceedings --- ?Ummid]ius Bassus, proconsul of the province [---]

Inscriptions commemorating governors mention that they brought in new revenues: Tiberius Plautius Silvanus Aelianus and Lucius Tampius Flavianus in the Balkans (LACTOR 8, 42 and 53); Rutilius Gallicus in Africa.

224 Statius, *Silvae* 1.4.83–6.
What of the wondrous obedience of Africans,
taxed though they are, and the triumph and glory you
earned in a peace so profound, and the riches so
great that not even the leader who sent you had
dared to look out for them?

Another new treasury, the Alexandrian (*Fiscus Alexandrinus*), appeared, perhaps to collect the monetary taxes of Egypt.

225 MW 202. Nomentum, near Rome.   To Ulpia Euhodia his excellent wife, Titus Flavius Delphicus, freedman of Augustus, clerk managing the account of the procurator in charge of the chests of inheritances of the Alexandrian treasury.

The collection of dues on goods passing in and out of the Empire gave rise to bureaucratic activity.

226 *Periplus of the Red Sea* 19.   On the left of Berenice after two or three days' run from Myos Hormos if you sail eastwards through the Gulf along the coast, there is a second harbour and port which is called Leuke Kome ('White Village'). This provides access to Petra and Malichas king of the Nabataeans. This has some means of trading for those who equip and dispatch ships of no great size to it from Arabia. Therefore it is the seat of a collector of the 25% tax on imported goods, and for the sake of security a centurion is settled there with a force.

The information from Egypt is particularly rich, but the following schedule is on stone rather than papyrus.

227 MW 459. Coptos, Egypt. 10 May 90. Greek.   According to the instructions [of Mettius Rufus, Governor of Egypt]. All that the tax gatherers of the toll-charge in Coptos that falls under the Arabarchy are to exact according to the schedule has been inscribed on this pillar through the agency of Lucius Antistius Asiaticus, prefect of Mount Berenice.

Red Sea steersman 8 drachmas; [---] 6 drachmas; officer in charge at the prow 10 drachmas; ?guard 10 drachmas; sailor 5 drachmas; repair man (ship's carpenter) 5 drachmas; artisan 8 drachmas; women for prostitution 108 drachmas; immigrant women 20 drachmas; women attached to soldiers 20 drachmas; ticket for camels 1 obol; sealing of a ticket 2 obols; outward journey of each ticket for a man going up 1 drachma; all women in general up to 4 drachmas; 1 donkey two obols; cart with a rectangular platform 4 drachmas; mast 20 drachmas; sailyard 4 drachmas; funeral procession being conveyed up and back again 1 drachma 4 obols. In the 9th year of Emperor Caesar [Domitian] Augustus [Germanicus]. 15th of the month Pachon.

The cost of Trajan's Dacian wars was high, but there were half a million Dacian prisoners also available for sale. Roman settlers took their place on the fertile soil, and the gold mines were for permanent exploitation; even so. Hadrian had his doubts.

228 Eutropius 8.6.2.   [Hadrian] was jealous of Trajan's glory and immediately abandoned three provinces that Trajan had acquired, recalling the armies of Assyria, Mesopotamia and Armenia, and intending the Euphrates to be the boundary of the Empire. He tried to do the same with Dacia, but his friends deterred him. to save many Romans being left to the mercy of the barbarians: on the conquest of Dacia Trajan had transferred boundless human resources there from the whole Roman world to cultivate the soil and create cities. For Dacia had been denuded of men by the long drawn out war of Decebalus.

Even Roman citizens could be targeted, and early in the Empire too: an unpopular tax on inheritances was introduced in 6 to finance the military treasury (*Aerarium militare*), to which only Roman citizens were liable, if they were celibate or childless, not to be eased until Trajan's reign.

229 Dio 55.25.1–5.   After this. during the consulships of Aemilius Lepidus and Lucius Arruntius, when no sources of income were being devised that pleased anyone. but rather one and all were disgruntled because an effort was actually being made, [25.2] Augustus contributed money to the treasury which he named the Military Treasury on his own behalf and on that of Tiberius ... [25.3] He himself contributed something and promised that he would do so every year, and accepted offers from kings and certain people. For from private individuals, willing though some of them were to give something (so they said), he took nothing. [25.4] Therefore, as these sums were minute in comparison with the enormous expenditures and there was need of some inexhaustible supply, he commissioned the senators to devise revenues, each individually and on his own account ... [25.5] However that may be, when they made various suggestions he approved none of them, but established the five per cent tax on whatever inheritances and legacies testators leave to people when they die, except to those who are close relatives or poor.

Nerva and Trajan won much credit for relaxing this rule.

230 Pliny, *Panegyric* 38.6 – 39.2.   Besides, when the Deified Nerva had ordained that children were necessarily free from paying the five per cent tax on the goods of their father, it was consistent that parents should secure the same immunity with regard to the property of their children: [38.7] why should the later generation be treated with greater respect than the earlier? why should the same principle of fairness not run backwards as well? You, Caesar, removed the condition, 'provided only that the son should have been under the paternal authority of the father'. You divined, I guess, the power of nature and its law which has ordered that children should always be under the power of their parents and, between humans, did not give power and the right to command to the stronger, as it did in the case of beasts. [39.1] Indeed, not content with having removed the first degree of relationship from the five per cent tax, he exempted the second grade as well, and provided that a brother in the case of his sister's goods and vice versa a sister in the case of her brother's, and a grandfather and grandmother in the case of their granddaughter and grandson's (and vice versa) should be kept free from tax. [39.2] To those too, who had become eligible for Roman citizenship through the Latin right, he allowed the same relaxation and granted the right of cognate relationships at a stroke to all without distinction and as nature does – a right which previous emperors were making a business of being asked for from individuals, not so much with the idea of granting it as of refusing.

Naturally, extravagance on the part of cities was discouraged, as in a letter to Munigua from Titus on their appeal against a judgement given against them by Sempronius Fuscus, proconsul 78–9, in favour of the tax farmer Servilius Pollio.

231 *AE* 1962, 288. Munigua, Baetica. 7 Sept. 79.   Emperor Titus Caesar Vespasian Augustus, Supreme Pontiff, in his ninth year of tribunician power, seven times consul, Father of the Fatherland gives greetings to the four-man board and councillors of Munigua. Since, then, you have appealed against paying the money that you owed to Servilius Pollio according to the judgement of Sempronius Fuscus, it was appropriate that the penalty for making an unjustified appeal should be exacted from you. But I have put what I say on the basis of my own forbearance rather than on your lack of prudence, and I have remitted the *HS* 50,000 to your treasury, given its fragile state, which you have offered in your own defence. I have written, moreover, to my friend Gallicanus, the proconsul, that the money that has been adjudged due to Pollio you shall pay, but that he should free you from payment of the interest from the day the judgement was delivered. It is fair that the income from your indirect taxes, which you indicate that Pollio had, should be taken into account, to prevent anything being lost to the community on this head. Farewell. Issued on the 7th day before the ides of September.

Under some emperors, beginning with Tiberius, the prosecution of wealthy persons for the advantage of prosecutor and state became notorious (for treason the proportion was 1:3 in favour of the state: Tacitus, *Ann.* 4.20.3). Hipparchus of Athens was prosecuted under Vespasian, unsuccessfully, then fatally under Domitian. (Cf. Suetonius, *Vesp.* 13.)

232 Philostratus, *Lives of the Sophists* 547–8. The sources of his (the sophist Herodes Atticus') wealth were numerous and came from several dynasties, but the greatest were those that came from his father and mother. For his grandfather Hipparchus had his property confiscated on the grounds that he was aiming at a tyranny. The Athenians did not bring this charge, but the emperor was not ignorant in the matter. The Goddess of Good Fortune, however, did not overlook the son of this man, Atticus, who was the father of Herodes, after he fell from wealth to poverty, but revealed to him something quite incalculable in the way of treasure in one of the houses that he had acquired near the theatre. Because it was so huge it made him more cautious rather than overjoyed. [548] He wrote the Emperor a letter in the following form: 'I have found treasure, my lord, on my own premises; what do you order me to do about it, then?' And the Emperor – it was Nerva who was in power at that time – replied, 'Use what you have found.' But Atticus remained just as cautious, and wrote that the size of the treasure was above him. 'Then misuse the windfall; it is yours.'

It was a merit noted in Trajan that he took his resources not from subjects but from the enemy.

233 Pliny, *Panegyric* 17.1. I have a vision now of a triumph loaded, not with the spoils of the provinces and gold extracted from our allies, but with enemy weapons and the chains of captured kings.

Individuals could enjoy their own property; and imperial sales (this time of Domitian's acquisitions) continued. (Cf. Suetonius, *Dom.* 3.2.)

234 Pliny, *Panegyric* 50.1–2, 5. But while we continue to enjoy your property as if it were ours as well, what we have remains so much our own property, so much ours! You do not enclose every pool, every lake, even every mountain pass, in a huge estate; rivers, mountains, seas are not enslaved to the enjoyment of a single pair of eyes. [2] There are things that Caesar looks at that do not belong to him, and the imperial power of the Emperor has eventually become greater than his private inheritance ... [5] An enormous placard is carried about bearing Caesar's name and a list of items for sale; that makes more detestable the greed of the person who lusted after so many things when he possessed so many that he did not need.

Mines, long a target for emperors in need (Tacitus, *Ann.* 6.19.1), were exploited to the full; Statius' address to the Dalmatian Vibius Maximus shows that by Domitian's time the Romans were below the superficial deposits and testing the schist below.

235   Statius, *Silvae* 4.7.13–16 *(with K. Coleman's note).*
When shall Dalmatian peaks allow
you back to lovely Latium? There
the white-faced miner looks on Wealth,
the god below the ground, and comes
from digging yellow as the gold.

Old workings were reopened.

236   Pliny, *Natural History* 34.164–5.   It is a unique fact about these (lead) mines that when they are abandoned they acquire a new lease of life and are more productive. [165] This seems to happen because air infiltrates the passages until they are completely full; it is the same with miscarriage, which seems to make some women more productive. This was recently discovered to be the case in Baetica, in the Salutariensian mine, which used to be leased out at two hundred thousand *denarii* a year. After it had fallen into disuse, it was leased for two hundred and fifty-five. Similarly the Antonian mine in the same province at the same leasing reached a rent of four hundred thousand.

Other imperial estates were intensely exploited, notably the balsam gardens of Judaea round Engedi and Jericho.

237   Pliny, *Natural History* 12.111–13.   But balsam is considered superior to every other scent. It is confined to Judaea alone of all countries. Formerly it was in only two gardens, each belonging to the king, one of them not more than twenty *iugera* in extent, the other smaller. The Emperors Vespasian and Titus displayed this species of shrub in the City. (It is a striking fact that since Pompey the Great we have carried even trees in our triumphs.) [112] This one is now in service as a slave and pays tribute along with the people to whom it belongs ... [113] The Jews vented their fury on it as they did on their own lives; the Romans by contrast defended it and there were fights to the death over a shrub. The imperial treasury now plants it and it has never been as widespread; its height has remained at a maximum of two cubits.

Planting of uncultivated ground on imperial estates was encouraged, as on the Villa Magna ('Great Farmstead') in Africa. The Mancian law, whether a formal enactment of the mid-first century or a practice devised by a landowner after whom it was named, encouraged the exploitation of derelict land by exempting it from rent for a certain period.

238   Inscription of Henchir Mettich. Sm. *N–H* 463, with D. Flach, *Chiron* 8 (1978) 477–84. 116–17.   [Column 1] [For] the safety of our Augustus Emperor Caesar Trajan, our leader, and for that of the entire Divine House, Optimus Germanicus Parthicus. Issued by Licinius Maximus and Felicior, freedman of Augustus, procurators, according to the precedent of the Mancian law.

Those who within the estate of Villa Magna Variana <?shall live> at Mappalia Siga are permitted to cultivate under the Mancian law those lands which were not included in the original allocation of lands on the estate in such a way that the person who cultivates them is to have use of them for his private purposes. From the crops which are brought forth there tenants shall be obliged to provide to the lord or lessees or to the managers of that estate, portions in accordance with the Mancian law, on the following terms: they are to render account on their own estimate to the lessees or managers of that estate of the products of each form of cultivation which they shall be obliged to bring to the threshing floor and thresh; and if they have given notice to the lessees or managers of that estate that <they> will give the tenant's share down to the smallest fraction, [within three days] they are to confirm on tablets the share of those crops down [to the smallest fraction] which they are obliged to [provide], to the lessees or managers [of that estate: the tenants] are to be obliged to provide the tenant's share on that basis.

Those who have or shall have domain farmsteads on the estate of Villa Magna or at Mappalia Siga shall be obliged to provide to the lords of that estate or to the lessees or their managers the shares down to the smallest fraction of the crops and vines, according to the Mancian practice, of each kind that they have: a third part of wheat from the threshing floor; a third part of barley from the threshing floor; of beans from the threshing floor a [fourth (or fifth)] part, of wine from the vat a third part, of pressed oil one third, of honey from the hive one *sextarius* from each hive. Anyone who has more than [Column 2] five hives at the time when the honey is or shall be gathered, shall be obliged to give [either] to the lord or to the lessees or managers of that estate a fifth [part] down to the smallest fraction. If anyone transfers hive, swarms, bees, honey-[pots] from the estate of Villa Magna or Mappalia Siga on to land outside the estate, so that either the lords or the lessees or managers of that <estate> ever suffer <?maximum> loss by fraud, those hives, swarms, bees, honey-pots, the honey which shall be brought in shall belong to the lessees or managers of that estate down to the smallest fraction.

As to dry fig trees [of that estate] which are outside the orchard, where the orchard is within the actual farmstead [so] that it does not extend more than [-] *iugera*, the tenant on his own estimate [shall be obliged to give] the lessees or managers of that estate a [third] share of the gathered crop. As to old fig and olive groves, which [were planted] before [this] law, [according to] custom he is to be obliged to provide crops to the lessee or managers of that <estate>. If any fig orchard is created from now on it is permitted for the person who planted it to pick the crop of that orchard for five successive harvests at his own discretion; after the fifth harvest he shall be obliged to provide the lessees or managers of that estate under the same law, as has been written out above. It is permitted to plant vines and cultivate them on the place of old vines on condition that at the next five vintages from that planting the person who thus planted them is to take the vintage at his own discretion and likewise after the fifth vintage after they were planted, a third part of the crop according to the Mancian law they shall be obliged to give to the lessees [Column 3] or [managers] of that <estate> down to the smallest fraction. It is permitted to plant an olive grove and cultivate it in that place in which someone has brought uncultivated land under cultivation, on condition that for the ten following olive harvests after that planting he is to be permitted from that planting to take the fruits of that olive grove which was planted in that manner; likewise that after <ten> harvests he shall be obliged to give to the lessees or managers of that [estate] a third part of the pressed oil. Anyone who has grafted wild olives shall after five [harvests] be obliged to provide one third. As to whatever grasslands there are or shall be on the estate of Villa Magna Variana [or] Mappalia Siga, except [those] lands which have vetches, the produce of those fields is to be given to the lessees or managers. Herdsmen shall be obliged to exact fees for sheep that graze within the estate of the Villa Magna (Mappalia Siga). For each head they shall be obliged to pay four *asses* to the lessees or managers of the lords of that estate.

If anyone from the estate of Villa Magna, or Mappalia Siga, cuts down a crop whether standing or on the tree, ripe or unripe, or digs it up or carries it away, carries it off, burns it, or lops it, it shall be for the tenant to [make up] the loss in the next two years to the lessees or managers; [Column 4] to the man on whom he [inflicted] the loss he shall be obliged to provide [the equivalent]. Any persons on the estate of Villa [Magna Variana or Mappalia Siga who] plant or shall plant [a fig orchard, olive grove, or vines are permitted to bequeath that area] by will [to their heirs] who have been or shall be born of a legitimate [marriage]. If any areas [after] this time have been or shall be given as a pledge [....] or in trust, the right of transferring the trust shall be preserved [for the heirs] under the Mancian law.

[As to any person who] puts an area under cultivation on land which has been uncultivated or shall do so, whether he who puts down or sites a building, or [if] he who [has cultivated it afterwards] abandons it and persists in abandoning it, at that time in which that area thus ceased to be cultivated or shall so cease, that area where there was or shall have been a right of cultivation, provided that it is preserved or shall be preserved for the next two-year period from the day on which it ceased to be cultivated, after the two year period is for the lessees or their managers. That area which was cultivated in the preceding year and shall have ceased to be cultivated, the lessee or manager of that estate is to make known to <the person to whom> that area is said to belong that on the evidence of witnesses he has persistently refused the cultivated area. Notification of the person of Mappalia Siga with witnesses, and likewise if he refuses for the following year, the lessees or the manager <of that estate> are to be required after a two-year period to cultivate that area without any grievance on his part.

No lessee or manager <of that estate> is to enjoin an inhabitant <of that estate> to provide <more than three double stints of work>. Tenants who live within the estate of Villa Magna or Mappalia Siga shall be obliged to provide masters or lessees [or their managers] to the smallest fraction every year two stints of ploughing for each man and two harvest stints, and two stints for activity of whatever kind. Tenants who are inhabitants of that estate are to hand in their names by [the day before the first day of each] year to the lessees or managers for one stint of guard duty each, which they have to provide in the countryside, reckoned separately [---] separately. As to hired security guards [who live within the estate of Villa Magna or] Mappalia Siga, they are to hand in their name for guard duties that they have to [provide] for the lessees or managers [of that estate]. Guard duties of the estate for slaves belonging to the owners [---] is [5 *fragmentary lines*] (*At bottom of Column 1*) This was inscribed by Lurius Victor, son of Odilo, master, and Flavius Geminus, advocate, and by Felix son of Annobal Birzil.

Even with the taxation on the most efficient footing possible, so that Vespasian could afford his advances in Germany and Britain, strain was put on frontiers and the financial system.

239 Dio 68.7.1.   (Trajan) spent huge sums on wars, and huge sums on works of peace; and although his constructions in respect of roads and harbours and public buildings were very numerous and absolutely essential he expended nobody's blood on any of them.

5.5. Trade and the Roman economy: the evidence from Pompeii and Ostia

The 'Roman economy' is a disputed concept, implying a unity that would mean that one part of the Empire could not be affected without this having an appreciable effect on another part, however distant. As one province might gain at the expense of another or independently of it, a 'cellular' economy is an attractive concept. However, the Empire was unified to some degree: politically, of course, and by a coinage operating almost universally throughout it, although local communities might be given permission to coin.

240 Sm. *G–N* 403. Bronze coin from Patrae, Achaea. *c.* 37. *Obverse.* Bust of Moneta, goddess of the mint, wearing a diadem and a veil. TO THE GOODNESS OF AUGUSTUS: GRANT OF A MINT.
   Reverse. Male figure holding an eagle-tipped sceptre, standing in a four-horse chariot. TO CAESAR AUGUSTUS, THE COLONY OF AROE AUGUSTA PATRAE.

The constant movement of travellers and dealers across the Empire, with minimal customs dues, also contributed to its unity. Workers travelled too.

241 *ILS* 7648. Lugdunum.   Sacred to the shades and eternal memory of Julius Alexander, a native of Africa, and a citizen of Carthage. He was an excellent man, a worker in the art of glass-blowing, who lived 75 years, five months and 13 days, without any hurtful act, with his wife Virginia, with whom he lived 48 years and on whom he begot three sons and a daughter; from all of these he knew grandchildren and he left them as survivors. This funeral monument was constructed under the supervision of Numonia Bellia his wife and Julius Alexaius his son and Julius Felix his son and Julius Gallonius his son and Numonia Belliosa his daughter, and likewise his grandsons Julius Auctus, Julius Felix Alexander, Julius Galonius, Julius Leontius, Julius Gal[---] and Julius Eonius in their devotion were responsible for it when it was in process of construction and dedicated it.

The roads of Italy were noticed as being particularly in need of repair under Trajan.

242 Galen 10.8, pp. 632–3 Kühn. But to put things in a nutshell, he (Hippocrates) seems to me to have laid down every road to cure, although to be sure it needs attention to become perfect. It is the same now. We see some of the routes across country – the old ones, which have come to have some part of them muddy or full of stones or scrub, steep and difficult or treacherously sloping, or infested with wild animals, or hard to pass because of great rivers, or long and rough. All the roads in Italy, in whichever of these conditions they were, the great Trajan put right. He paved the flooded and muddy parts with stone, or raised them on high banks, cleaning out the scrubby and rough parts and throwing bridges over rivers that were difficult to ford. And where the route was longer than appropriate he cut another, shorter. In the same way if a road was difficult because of the height of a summit he diverted it through easier country. And if the way led through country infested with wild animals or a desert, he turned the route away from there and directed it through populous areas, smoothing out rough places.

Some provinces, especially Baetican Spain, the Gauls and the Province of Asia, began to overtake Italy in economic prosperity. The Roman army, based in the provinces, was paid from taxation raised there. The army paid its way by constituting a market for food, clothing and weapons. Hence money tended to move round the provinces rather than be transported to Italy. Italian producers would be hard put to benefit from these distant markets, and the Roman Peace was allowing the provinces to develop their own crops and manufactures, notably wine and pottery.

The potteries at Condatomagus (La Graufesenque) were already working under Tiberius and produced enormous quantities of material, more than a million vessels, of which the common types included in the lists below account for more than 96%. Graffiti on sherds used as dockets from there reveal the numbers of each kind of pot made by individual Gaulish workers, some of whom have recognisably Roman names; the shapes of the pots listed are subjects of discussion.

243 *Graffites* **119, no. 3 (Neronian date).**

Tuth[os]		
Cornutos	jars at two thirds of a foot	[---]
	baskets	300
	one foot jars	90
	mortars	125
	mortars	100
	dishes	850
	ink pots	260
Scota with Felix	dishes	5500
Trito(s) with Privatos	cups	7200
Deprosagi	drinking vessels	2500
Masuetos	mugs	3700
	wine cups	9000

Shippers on the rivers of Gaul are often commemorated.

244 *ILS* **7032. Lugdunum.** Gaius Julius Sabinus, shipper on the Rhône, presented in honour of the Rhône shippers.

Italy was not in the economic van, and luxuries had to be paid for, to the advantage of exporters such as Arabia Felix ('Happy').

245 Pliny, *Natural History* 12.82–4. What has made it 'happy' is the extravagance of human beings even in death, when they burn over the deceased spices that they knew perfectly well to have been created for the benefit of the gods. [83] Writers who know their business repeatedly claim that Arabia does not produce as much in its annual crop as the Emperor Nero threw into the flames for his wife Poppaea at her death. You can go on to work out the total number of funerals every year and the piling up into heaps in honour of corpses of materials that are offered to the gods in single granules ... [84] But the Arabian Sea is even 'happier': out of it come the pearls that it exports; and on the lowest estimate a hundred million sesterces every year are taken from us by India, the Chinese and that peninsula of Arabia. That is the high price of our fancy tastes and our women. For what proportion of those items, I ask you, now goes on anything to do with the gods of the underworld?

The main ports for Rome were Ostia and Puteoli; it was concern for the vital supplies of Rome, notably grain, that made Claudius improve the harbour of Ostia (Dio 60.11.1–5 = LACTOR 15, pp. 92–3). His works were inadequate, and 200 grain ships were lost there in 62 (Tacitus, *Ann.* 15.18.3; see **253** below for an association of divers). Improvements were carried out and recorded on coins of 112–14 (LACTOR 8, 92; cf. Pliny, *Ep.* 6.31.15) and epigraphically.

246 Sm. *N–H* 384. Ostia. 112–17. [To Emperor Caesar] Trajan [?Optimus Augustus Germanicus Dacicus ?Parthicus] Supreme Pontiff, [in his - year of tribunician power, hailed Imperator - times], six times [consul], Father of the Fatherland, [---] of the harbour of Traianus Felix

There was a Forum Vinarium ('Vintners' market') at Ostia, but a multiplicity of occupations and interests is obvious.

247 *ILS* 6146. To Gnaeus Sentius Felix, son and grandson of Gnaeus, of the Terentian tribe, coopted into the rank of ex-aedile by decree of the city council, coopted into the city council by decree of the council, quaestor in charge of the city treasury of Ostia, duovir, quaestor supervising the young men. This man was the first who, in the year in which he was coopted as a member of the city council, both became quaestor of the treasury and was designated to the duovirate for the following year. He was quinquennial curator of sea-going ships; coopted without charge into the corporation of seamen of the Adriatic Sea, and into the association situated at the post at the four-horse chariot in the Vintners' market, patron of the band of clerks who work in wax tablets and of copyists and of lictors and attendants; likewise of heralds and silversmiths and of City businessmen in the wine trade; likewise of the assessors of grain under the patronage of the Augustan Ceres; likewise of the corporation of boatmen and ferrymen at Lucullus' Crossing, and of the Tree-Bearers and citizens in the market and at the public weighing machine, and of the freedmen and public slaves, and of the dealers in olives and of the young men ?driving two-wheelers for hire, and of the Augustan veterans, likewise of the men attached to the service of Augustus' grain procurator, and of the fishermen selling their own catch; curator of the young men's show. Gnaeus Sentius Lucilius Gamala Clodianus, to his most kindly father.

Trajan concerned himself with other harbours as well.

248 Sm. *N–H* 387. Arch at Ancona. 114–15. To Emperor Caesar Nerva Trajan Optimus Augustus, son of the deified Nerva, Germanicus Dacicus, Supreme Pontiff, in his nineteenth year of tribunician power, hailed Imperator nine times, six times consul, Father of the Fatherland, leader with supreme foresight, the senate and Roman People (has dedicated this) because he has rendered the approach to Italy safer for mariners by adding this harbour too at his own expense. [*left*] To Plotina Augusta, the spouse of Augustus. [*right*] To the deified Marciana, the sister of Augustus.

In the first-century business world of the Sulpicii of Puteoli, grain might be used as security on a loan, as an item from their archives shows. It belongs to the dossier relating to the grain merchant Lucius Marius Jucundus; the manager of the Barbatian Granaries, privately owned by Nero's aunt Domitia Lepida, was P. Annius Seleucus, of which no. 26 was hired for 100 sesterces per month; Jucundus had deposited grain there and offered it to Sulpicius Faustus as security on a loan of *HS* 20,000 obtained by Faustus (*Tabulae Pompeianae* 53). It would seem that the manager is weighing out all the grain to control the amount (Camodeca on *TPSulp* 79), not just the 100 sesterces' worth each month for rent.

249 *TPSulp* 124, no. 46. 13 March 40. [Note in the hand of Nardus, slave of Publius Annius Seleucus], on the hiring of Granary 26 [---] Publius Annius [Seleucus]. In the consulships of Gaius Laecanius [Bassus and Quintus Terentius Culle]o, [on the third day before the ides of March]. I, Nardus, [the slave of] Publius [Annius Seleucus, have written this out] in the presence of and on the orders of [Publius Annius Seleucus] my [master], because [he declared] that he [could not read or write]: [I hired out] to Gaius Sulpicius [Faustus] Granary [26, which is included] in the upper [Barbatian estate of Domitia] Lepida; in [this granary is deposited thirteen] thousand [*modii* of Alexandrian wheat which] my [master] will measure out with [his slaves] for a fee each month of a hundred sesterces. (*Seals*) Transacted at Puteoli. Seals of Publius Annius Seleucus, Gnaeus Julius Felix, Nardus, slave of Publius Annius Seleucus, Publius Annius Seleucus.

A system of perpetual loans to farmers, the interest to be paid for the support of children of the Italian country towns, was at least a gesture in the direction of encouraging the birthrate, which had been a topic of anxiety since the mid-second century BC.

250 Sm. *N–H* 436. Veleia, Liguria. 102–14. Mortgage on estates for the sum of *HS* 1,044,000, so that from the beneficence of our best and greatest leader, Emperor Caesar Nerva Trajan Augustus Germanicus Dacicus, boys and girls may receive money for their maintenance: legitimate boys to the number of 245 receiving *HS* 16 (monthly) each, making a total of *HS* 47,040; legitimate girls to the number of 34 receiving *HS* 12 (monthly) each, making a total of *HS* 4896; illegitimate boy, 1 at *HS* 144 (annually); illegitimate girl, 1 at *HS* 122 (annually). Total *HS* 52,200, which comes to 5 per cent of the allocation written out above.

[Col. 1: first of nearly fifty mortgages] Gaius Volumnius Memor and Volumnia Alce, acting through Volumnius Diadumenus, their freedman, declared the Quintiacus Aurelianus estate, the Muletas hill with its woods, which is in the Ambitrebian parish at Veleia, and which has as its neighbours Marcus Mommeius Pericus, Satrius Severus, and public property: *HS* 108,000. They are due to receive *HS* 8692 and to pledge the estate above mentioned.

The great estates (*latifundia*) for which Italy is notorious – in spite of the survival of small and moderate-sized farms in favourable areas – spread to the provinces: Pliny uses the word and alludes to Virgil, *Georgics* 2.412.

251 Pliny, *Natural History* **18.35.**   The ancients thought that keeping the size of a farm moderate was a prime consideration; certainly they maintained a view to the effect that it was better to sow less arable land and plough it better. (I see that Virgil was also of this opinion.) And to speak candidly, huge estates have ruined Italy and now they are ruining the provinces too. Six landowners used to possess half Africa, when Nero killed them. Gnaeus Pompeius should not be cheated of this aspect of his greatness either: he never bought land that was adjoining his own.

A boundary stone shows that the colony of Capua in Campania owned land on Crete (assigned to it to make up for loss in Italy.

252 *AE* 1969/70, 635. Archanes in the territory of Knossos. 84 (*and mentioning a known duovir of that colony, Plebeius, who was acting for it*).   When Emperor Domitian Caesar Augustus Germanicus was consul for the tenth time, boundary stones were set up under the direction of Publius Messius Campanus, procurator of Caesar, between the Flavian Augustan Colony of Felix Capua and Plotius Plebeius, [in accordance with] the decision of Emperor Titus Augustus and with the agreement of both sides.

To even up matters between Italy and the provinces (and to release land for arable farming), Domitian's vine edict ordered the destruction of half the vines in the provinces and banned replanting in Italy. (Cf. Suetonius, *Dom.* 7.2, and 14.)

253 Philostratus, *Lives of the Sophists* **520.**   The embassies to the Emperor of which he (the sophist Scopelian) was a member were numerous; a degree of good fortune used to accompany him on his embassies, but the most successful was on behalf of the vines, when he was sent, not only on behalf of the people of Smyrna, as on most of his embassies, but for the whole of Asia at once. I shall reveal the purpose of the embassy: the Emperor's view was that Asia should not have any vines, because he thought that men became seditious under the influence of drink; the existing vines were to be uprooted, and others were not to be planted any more. What was needed was a joint embassy and a man who was going to use his charm on their behalf like another Orpheus or Thamyris. Accordingly they all chose Scopelian, and he was more than successful on the mission, so much so that he came back in possession not only of permission to plant, but with actual penalties to be imposed on those who were failing to do so.

A little after Gnaeus Sentius Saturninus, who did so well out of Adriatic shipping and the wine trade, another member of the Ostian upper class displays connexions with Africa: Hippo Regius was a centre of the corn trade, and the man's tribe, Quirina, suggests that his family may even have originated from there.

254 *CIL* 14, Suppl. 4620. To Publius Aufidius Fortis, son of Publius, of the Quirina tribe, by decree of the city council adlected duovir, four times [quaestor] of the treasury of the people of Ostia, prefect of the carpenters at Ostia, patron of the associations of grain assessors and divers, adlected member of the city council at Hippo Regius in Africa: the Association of merchants in grain; quinquennial magistrate for an indefinite period.

CHRONOLOGICAL LIST OF EMPERORS

AD 14:	19 Aug.	Death of Augustus, leading to sole rule of Tiberius
37:	16 Mar.	Death of Tiberius, followed by accession of Gaius Caligula
41:	22 Jan.	Assassination of Gaius Caligula, followed by accession of Claudius
54:	13 Oct.	Death of Claudius, followed by accession of Nero
68:	8 June	Suicide of Nero, followed by accession of Galba
69:	15 Jan.	Assassination of Galba, followed by accession of Otho
	15 Apr.	Suicide of Otho, followed by accession of Vitellius
	21 Dec.	Murder of Vitellius, followed by recognition of Vespasian
79:	24 June	Death of Vespasian, leaving Titus in sole power
81:	13 Sept.	Death of Titus, leading to accession of Domitian
96:	18 Sept.	Assassination of Domitian, followed by accession of Nerva
97:	end of Oct.	Adoption of Trajan
98:	?27 Jan.	Death of Nerva, leaving Trajan as sole ruler
117:	?7 Aug.	Death of Trajan
	11 Aug.	Hadrian recognised as Emperor, in Antioch

CONCORDANCE

(by document number)

A. Literary Sources

B. Inscriptions, Coins and Papyri

INDEXES
(by page)

1. Index of Persons
(including deities; emperors in CAPITALS, well known persons by their familiar names, other Romans by gentile names)

2. Index of Places (with modern equivalents) and Peoples

3. General Index

Printed in the United States
by Baker & Taylor Publisher Services